GUILT
IS
GOOD!

What Working Moms Need To Know

Muriel S. Savikas, Ph. D.

Parenting 101
www.parenting101.com

GUILT IS GOOD
What Working Moms Need to Know

By Muriel Savikas, Ph. D.

Published By:
Parenting 101
868 Manhattan Beach Blvd., Ste. 3
Manhattan Beach, CA 90266

For reasons of privacy, the names of all interviewed mothers have been changed.

Printed in the United States of America
1 2 3 4 5 6 7 8 9 10

ISBN: 0-9657741-6-3
Library of Congress Catalog Number: 97-92543

ABOUT THE AUTHOR

Dr. Muriel Savikas is a Professional Mediator and Child Psychologist in private practice in Manhattan Beach, California. Dr. Savikas is an advocate for children. She specializes in problematic issues of emotional and behavioral development of infants, toddlers, preschoolers and children by incorporating a multifaceted approach to therapy and training for parents and teachers. As Director of the Counseling and Mediation Institute, Dr. Savikas conducts divorce mediations, child custody evaluations, consults to the court regarding children's issues, serves as child development expert witness, provides psychological and neuropsychological testing, parent education, and therapy. She speaks widely to groups and organizations on divorce and communication topics pertaining to young children. She has published numerous featured articles and columns and has been interviewed for nationwide newspapers. Her book *Guilt is Good: What Working Moms Need to Know* has resulted from her work and interviews with working mothers. She is step-mom to three children.

TABLE OF CONTENTS

To Mom

CHAPTER 1

WHERE IT ALL BEGAN

Our parents cast long shadows over our lives. When we grow up, we imagine that we can walk in the sun, free of them. We don't realize, until it's too late, that we have no choice in the matter; they're always ahead of us.

— *Richard Eyre*

* * *

There's an old saying: "No matter where you go, there you are." And when it comes to families, nothing could be more true. The physical characteristics you inherit from your forebears are obvious; however, the emotional traits handed down to you are much less apparent and often become evident only when you are under stress or when someone brings one of them to your attention either out of love or malice.

Our sense of self starts with our upbringing. You take your first steps, say your first words, and have most of your significant early experiences within the confines of your family home. Your deepest sense of value and self-worth—or the lack of it— developed from the relationship you had with your parents. Like it or not, their responses helped determine how you felt about yourself as a child and now as an adult.

FOLLOWING IN YOUR FAMILY'S FOOTSTEPS

Your parents' influence is there with you every day. It's easiest to notice in the little things. You go to a grocery store to buy a box of cereal. Maybe you decide to try something new. But, as you reach for that new box, you see the familiar Quaker Oats—the one your father always ate—next to it. And you can almost hear him say, "Stick with what you know."

In the middle of the afternoon, your child is playing in the yard. Her brightly-colored ball rolls out into the street and she runs after it. You would probably have said it anyway, but you hear your mother's voice, as you yell, "Don't run out into the street!" You know the anxiety that kind of warning caused you as a child, how hearing the word "don't" made you feel like you were going to fail no matter what you did. But the words burst out of your mouth just the same.

We re-enact the positive too. Late at night, when you tuck your kids into bed, you may find yourself kissing their foreheads like your mother did or singing them the quaint old campfire song you loved to hear your father sing before you fell asleep.

If you decide to keep in touch or never speak to your family again, the imprint of your family is hard to shake. It defines your world. The experiences you lived through together—whether nurturing or conflicted, painful or secure—have become an indelible part of you. Wherever you go, there they are.

✳ ✳ ✳

WHAT WAS IT LIKE IN YOUR FAMILY?

"For awhile when I was growing up, my mom ran an antique store. She was always selling off our furniture and bringing things home from the shop. Sometimes we had lawn chairs in the living room; sometimes old Victorian antiques. I thought everybody's mom did that."

— Carey

* * *

When you're growing up, it takes awhile to realize that other people's families are different from your own. Even after you discover this, the patterns of your own family set the standard. Good or bad, your family's own habits seem like the most natural. Anything else is *unfamiliar* (a word that means "not like family"). Change is possible, but it feels like a risk. Whether you feel guilty about the things you choose to do or not to do usually results from the kind of messages you learned long ago about making decisions. Even if you were taught to make your own decisions and choose your own path, you may still be under the influence of your parents and the decisions they made.

Starting your own family means asking yourself important questions that are not always easy to answer:

✿ Where will I live?

✿ How many children will I have?

✿ Will I work full-time?

✿ What will I do about childcare?

✿ Who will be a part of my life?

Responsibility lies squarely on your shoulders now. If it is heavily influenced by your family patterns (that voice in your head, nudging you this way and that) you might just follow the path your parents chose. However comfortable and "right" that may feel, it may not prove to be the best for you. Their circumstances at the time, their expectations and their own personalities influenced their decisions. In your life, the choice is up to you. But, whether you feel guilty about the things you choose has a lot to do with the kind of messages you heard during your developmental years.

✳ ✳ ✳

WHAT WERE THE MESSAGES
IN YOUR FAMILY?

"When I was in high school, my dad came home from work at 3 p.m. It seems hard to believe, now, but we got dressed up every day and stood waiting at the door for him. I think we were imitating the Donna Reed show. We thought it was right if they did it on TV."

— Anne

Every woman plays a variety of roles in her life. Within your family, you may be a wife, mother, friend, and lover. In the outside world, you may play the role of entrepreneur, employee, student, committee member, teacher and friend.

Playing a lot of roles may offer you a full, satisfying life. By putting on new hats, you may find yourself more flexible, more open to change and growth.

Family problems often occur because of the roles its members are playing. Children or parents may begin to play inappropriate roles or roles not suited to their temperament. Sometimes, they may be locked into a role they have outgrown.

In my sessions with working moms, I have heard women tell the countless and varied roles they played in their birth families. I have seen how strongly those roles can influence the present. Reacting to her upbringing, Deborah unwittingly married a man with the same prejudice against women that her father had.

"My father wouldn't let my mother work till I was in high school; and then, she could only work in the school cafeteria part-time. I thought I would be much more self-sufficient, but once I married, my husband had the same agenda. He wanted me barefoot and pregnant. 'It's still a man's world,' he said. 'You should stay at home.'"

— Dolores

When the roles are rigid, children cannot develop appropriately and parents are unnecessarily locked into authoritarian roles. In families like this, the unexpected twists and turns of life are often seen as a threat. Usually, no one says it out loud, but the silent message is: "Be careful! It's a dangerous world out there. And we can't handle it."

In a flexible family the members have better shock absorbers and unpredictable events are less stressful. Instead of stiffly resisting every bump, they are more relaxed when riding on difficult roads. When challenges do arise, they have more options at their disposal. Parents who set this kind of tone in a family are telling their children: "Whatever comes up, we can handle it. We are here for you."

❋ ❋ ❋

Unspoken Cues

Children are always alert for unspoken cues. They learn their family's messages by heart.

"It wasn't what my parents' said that got to me—it was their lack of affection. They were so caught up in their own lives that they didn't have time for me. I took it for granted that I was in the way, an inconvenience. They never told me otherwise."

—Karly

* * *

MESSAGES WE TAKE FOR GRANTED

In the family where you grew up, what were the unspoken messages:

✿ about you?

✿ your parents?

✿ your family?

✿ mothers outside the family?

Are you living by your own beliefs about priorities and change, or by the ones you learned at home?

* * *

Messages About You

"Everyone assumed I'd marry and have kids. But my father always told me that he wanted me to be financially secure —just in case. His marriage had lasted, but you could never be sure. Without even thinking about my reasons, I opened my own business before I got married. I followed his advice to the letter."

— Wanda

* * *

"Don't Help Me!"

When Deanie was five, her mother developed breast cancer. From the time she was eight, Deanie did all the shopping and baby-sitting for her mother and her younger brother. Six years later, her mother died.

At first, Deanie and her brother were sent to live with an aunt so oppressive that they still call her "the slave driver." Soon afterward, they were shunted into foster care. When her absent father showed up one day, he picked up her brother but left Deanie behind. "I have never understood the purpose of men," Deanie says today. "I didn't realize how much other women depend on them till I was an adult. I will never let anyone else take responsibility for me."

* * *

High Society

Joy was sent away to boarding school when she was ten. A few years earlier, her father had been disabled by a heart attack. She missed being his beloved caretaker when she was at school, but he regularly sent her affectionate notes and gifts. It seemed clear that her mother had only had a child to please him. She took little interest in Joy herself. Her mother was a social butterfly, who spent her time decorating houses and flitting from one party to another. Both parents were so certain that Joy would marry into status after finishing school that they didn't even bother to give her a middle name. "You'll use your maiden name," they said.

* * *

Pleasing Daddy

Jacki's mother abdicated the care of the four younger siblings to Jacki. It fell to her to rush home after school to baby-sit the kids—which meant she had no outside friends or activities. Tired of the job, Jacki put off starting a family of her own. When she got pregnant at nineteen, she gave the child up for adoption. At twenty-four, she had a quick abortion. She followed it at *thirty-three with a fortuitous miscarriage. By then, she was ready. At thirty-five and thirty-eight, she gladly bore two children.*

Although Jacki saw herself as a singer and an actress, her parents couldn't see beyond her early role as a parent. She remembers her father saying, over and over again, "I'll be glad when you girls get married." As if to please him, she and all her sisters have each been married three times!

* * *

Messages About Family

"I was the baby of the family and I always felt I was jostling for position. It seemed to me that all the strokes went to my older siblings, who were better at getting my parents' attention. Since I couldn't get them to notice me at home, I worked extra hard at school. I graduated valedictorian and that impressed them — briefly."

— Charlene

The dynamics between parent and child in a family can take many forms. Sometimes both parents focus their attention on the child. At other times, one parent may side with the child. The energy is constantly shifting.

Salvador Minuchin, who devoted his career to the study of families, said that it was not uncommon for parents to use their child as a way to avoid their own problems or in their relationship with one another.

Whenever someone asserts his or her individuality, people in the family notice. A father takes up sailing, a mother opens a pastry shop or a child shows promise in science—all of these activities give the individual an identity and may be sewn like emblems into the family tapestry.

Myth making begins with these new labels and they can generate a strong sense of pride—in the individual and the family alike. ("Everyone knows mom's a whiz in business." "My girl's going to be the next Madam Curie!") Knowing that a certain quality is undisputed in her family, the individual can cultivate it with confidence.

On the other hand, a destructive myth can do serious damage to a child's self-esteem. If Jesse comes in second place and is told "You should've caught that ball!" the underlying message is: "You're a loser!" With that belief firmly entrenched in his mind, there is a good chance he will continue to feel like a loser, even when he wins.

Myths can be self-fulfilling prophesies—whether they build up confidence or tear it down. If someone is no longer free to be herself, the expectation of the myth has become an unreasonable demand.

Many of the working moms I've spoken to still wince when remembering those myths.

* * *

FAMILY MYTHS

Think about the family myths relating to you.

❧ What is the myth about you that first comes to your mind?

❧ What is the myth your mother always mentions?

❧ What is the myth your father always mentions?

❧ Do you believe the myth is true?

❧ Can you risk letting go of the myth?

❧ What would happen if you did?

In *Parenting by Heart*, Dr. Ron Taffel says that parents often feel self-conscious and incompetent because of their image of a perfect parent Even though no one has achieved perfect parenthood yet, these unrealistic expectations are passed from generation to generation.

Messages About Parents

"I waited a long time to have a child. When Melissa was born, I was overjoyed. As a single parent, I knew there'd be a lot of things to juggle, but I guess I thought I'd just become an efficiency expert. Instead, I do a little of this, a little of that. It feels like I never have time to do anything well!"

—Marci

To compound the situation, what was true in previous generations is not necessarily true today. In another time, mothers staying home with their kids was the norm. But according to a recent *USA Today* poll, 61 percent of mothers in America work. Without taking current realities into account, outdated messages about parenting can result in frustration and guilt. And, as we will see, many of these supposed ideals are not so ideal after all.

THE "PERFECT MOM" MYTH

According to this myth, the Perfect Mom:

✿ always has time for her kids

✿ never gets angry or yells

✿ is wise and resourceful

✿ knows what to do in a crisis

✿ spends quality time with her child every day

✿ is mature and self-sufficient

✿ makes the child the center of her reality

✿ stays in charge of the family at all times

✳ ✳ ✳

FAMILY PATTERNS

One Parent-Child Team

When Todd reached adolescence, Marie was glad to see her husband spending more time with him. The two began to play more vigorous games of football on the lawn. On weekends, they started going fishing or to baseball games regularly. Marie felt increasingly left out. When she asked to go along, Todd said these were "manly things" and, looking at his dad for support, made a joke about women.

While a parent may sometimes become an advocate for the child spending too much time with one parent, the child gives the other parent the message, "It's 2 against 1."

When a child is born into a family, he or she needs constant attention. All other priorities are set aside for the baby's needs. But as the child grows, the parents in a healthy family begin to participate more in the outside world, and the child is no longer their primary focus.

By gradually directing their concerns to their lives outside the family, parents teach their child how to live day to day in a world where they are not—and have no need to be—the center of attention.

✳ ✳ ✳
Child-Focused

A few years ago, Suzanne and Bill were thinking about a divorce. They had been married seven years and seemed to have nothing in common any more. Then little Charlie got sick. The doctors couldn't understand what it was at first. So they both spent weeks going back and forth with Charlie to the hospital for tests. Even after the danger was over and Charlie was released with medication, Suzanne and Bill talked only about Charlie's health. The issues surrounding their relationship were not addressed and Charlie became the "glue" that held the marriage together.

THE DYNAMICS OF THE PARENT-CHILD RELATIONSHIP

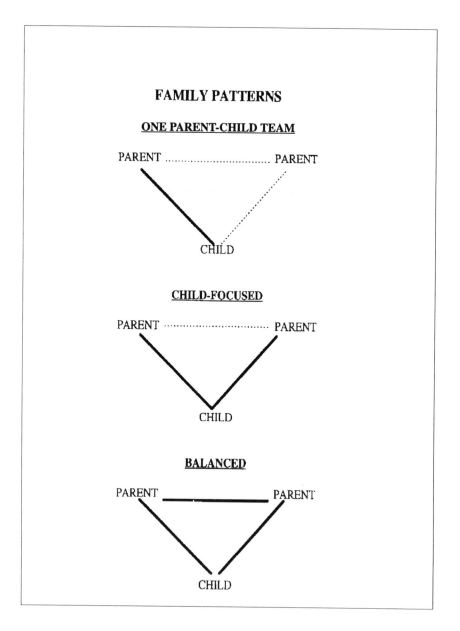

FAMILY PATTERNS

ONE PARENT-CHILD TEAM

PARENT .... PARENT

CHILD

CHILD-FOCUSED

PARENT .... PARENT

CHILD

BALANCED

PARENT _____ PARENT

CHILD

Ultimately, a child in Charlie's position learns to manipulate his parents by playing on their fears. And, in Charlie's case, he might learn the psychological power of using an illness to gain attention. Sadly, he is only doing what they taught him by their own behavior—using their anxiety to meet his needs.

* * *

Balanced

On Tuesday, Caryn had a bad day at school. The boy she thought was going to ask her to the junior high school dance asked someone else instead. When she got home, she snapped at her mom. Her father sternly sent her to her room without dinner. But when her mother explained why Caryn was upset, he changed his mind and put some dinner on a plate for her.

When there is a balance, the energy flows naturally between family members, adjusting to personalities and levels of stress from day to day. There is a natural give and take.

FAMILY FOCUS

Ask yourself:

❀ Who was the focus of attention in your family when you were growing up?

❀ How did that focus change? Were you comfortable or uneasy with that focus?

❀ Can you see it being repeated in your own family now?

❀ How is your own family balance different?

---

* * *

Messages About Others

"I never saw my parents go to a movie together or a social event of any kind. The only friends that came by for supper were relatives—many of whom we didn't even like! I got the feeling that, once you married and had kids, that was it. The only world outside the front door after that was work."

— Bobbi

＊ ＊ ＊

Just as relationships between members of a family can get locked into a pattern, so can relationships between the family and others. As you may expect, a parent who relies too strongly on a child to meet his or her needs is unlikely to have a satisfying life outside the family. On the other hand, when a parent has a wide variety of friends and connections, there is less strain on the family itself.

In an unhealthy family—one where parents regularly side with one another against their child, or one parent sides with a child against her spouse—the flow between the family and the outside world is blocked. Family loyalty becomes the highest priority. There may be a desperate fear of revealing family secrets. In extreme cases, even confiding in a friend can be seen as a betrayal. The wrong message is, "If you share love, you lose it."

By contrast, a healthy family is the center for a virtual network of connections. As each member meets new people, the network changes and grows. The parents teach discretion about certain family matters, but the mood is open and inviting. Paradoxically, each member in an open family feels more secure. By including others, they extend their circle of connectedness and love.

CHAPTER 2

DO I LOOK GUILTY?

While working itself does not seem to bring harm to our children,
the guilt we feel over it certainly does.

— Barbara Berg

We live in an exciting time of transition. In the last 30 years, Americans have made an exodus—moving from small, rural communities to live in cities with millions of people. We have landed on the moon and created a global village on the worldwide web. Instead of sharing one, gas-guzzling vehicle, we now average 2.1 economy cars for every 1.9 adults. We own three TVs per family and—if we opt to buy our own satellite dish—we have access to hundreds of different channels.

No one ever offered our parents a satellite dish or a zippy little import when we were growing up. Microwaves, computers and ATMs were the futuristic gadgets of science fiction. After the hardships of the Great Depression, the atrocities of World War II, and the fear of nuclear war, the typical housewife was said to be eager to spend her days at home, quietly feathering the nest. If she longed for a more stimulating career, she kept it to herself. From all appearances, housewives had no corporate ambitions whatsoever. This was the mindset generally portrayed in TV shows like Ozzie and Harriet where the wife was the happy home-maker.

Today, we love our children no less than Harriet loved David and Ricky, but today the context is radically different — less than 36 percent of moms stay home until their children reach adulthood. Few of us can afford to stay home and more of us realize that we don't want to.

For too long now, working moms have blamed themselves for not being the mom in an apron, standing at the front door, waiting for her hubby to return. That vision formed by TV shows and/or our own experience—what we saw our own mothers do while we were growing up—is a role that doesn't apply any more, but its very existence, in the back of our minds, can make us feel guilty.

✳ ✳ ✳

ABOUT NOT BEING SUPER MOM

"Three months after Jason was born, I went back to work full-time. The job is only 40 hours a week, but the commute adds another 10. By the time I pick him up from the after school care, I barely have time to cook dinner, give him a bath, help him with his homework and tuck him into bed. It's not what I call quality time. And I'm exhausted all day long!"

— Sherry

Without knowing it, many working moms live by an unwritten code that says they must give 100 percent of themselves to work *and* 100 percent of themselves to their kids. This code doesn't allow for compromise or balance between the roles.

When faced with a choice between spending quality time with her son on his science projects and finishing a job for her boss,

Sandy, like many of us, doesn't try to prioritize one over the other. "I just stay up all night and do both," she says.

This is the fast track to burn-out. Instead of feeling empowered, a working mom who hasn't learned to adapt her expectations to the realities of her life feels defeated no matter what she does. Before her daughter was born, Jan had invested eight years in a law firm with ambitions to be a partner within a few years. She didn't think being a mother would make a difference, but once she had a baby, she realized she would have to give up her dream. "When I'm home, my daughter follows me around the house. By Sunday night, it's a bit much. But it makes me realize she needs more mommy-time with me. I guess I'll cut back on my hours again. I've really had to sell myself short in my career to have more flexible time with her."

Driven by guilt, some working moms stop attending to their own needs and attend to everyone else's. Even if the task is impossible, they feel they have to try because, according to the unwritten code, "they will only have themselves to blame if they can't do it all."

"One of the worst moments I had with my son," Diane recalled, "was when he asked me what he had been like as a baby. I had been so busy rushing back and forth from work to daycare, trying to cook and shop and manage our lives, that I couldn't remember! I felt so guilty. I thought, *this is the kind of thing a mom ought to know. A real mom would be able to remember!*"

Working moms spend their time doing so many things at once they rarely stop to give themselves enough credit for what they *are* accomplishing!

Sharon has two adopted kids. Her corporate job requires her to travel a lot. When she does come home, she is eager to find ways to spend quality time with her kids, but she is often too tired to do the things she'd like with them. "I don't have the energy to learn the computer games they want me to play. I usually resort to telling them a story I've made up instead."

Because she hasn't met her own expectations of what a mother should do, Sharon feels frustrated and inadequate. In reality, her kids may be much more satisfied by a personal story than one ready-made in a book. It is little things like that that make quality time so precious. It is not the activity as much as the care with which it's done.

The secret to squeezing in a few moments of quality time in a hectic week is to limit the time of the activity beforehand. After dinner and an early bath, you might say, "It's 6:00. Your bedtime is at 8:00. So, we have two whole hours. What would you like to do?" Be sure to pick a project that is not chore-oriented (like cleaning up a room together) but one that will be enjoyable to both of you. (If you can't endure watching a Disney movie for the fortieth time, it's better to suggest something else.)

However, another focus of quality time can be sharing with one another when chores *are* necessary. For example, sharing clean-up time, or washing and drying dishes can be very special times if you and your child discuss the things that each of you experienced throughout the day. Chores become less chore-like when they become sharing experiences.

❋ ❋ ❋

THE SEARCH FOR QUALITY TIME

Quality time is where you find it.

Whether you are spending the day with your child or rushing through your week, it is important to connect with your child at several key moments throughout the day. According to Dr. Sirgay Sanger, the most important ones are:

✿ *in the morning, when the child wakes up*

✿ *on leaving for work*

✿ *at the mid-morning check-in call*

✿ *on coming home*

✿ *at dinner*

✿ *during shared time*

✿ *at bath and bedtime*

✿ *if the child wakes up in the night*

ABOUT WANTING A CAREER TOO

For Yourself

"I love my kids, but I want to continue my career. Before they were born, I had invested ten years, paying my dues in advertising. Their father is a copywriter and he's not giving up his job. Now that I'm the head of my department, why should I give up mine?"

— Sonja

The guilt that follows on the heels of genuine ambition is often hidden. Even with the confidence that comes with success, a working mom who has a strong investment in her career can suffer from a nagging uneasiness. She may ask herself, "What kind of mom am I, if I find my job as satisfying as raising my kids?"

"There was this whole thing for me about leaving my baby in someone else's hands," Lynn said. "I felt extremely anxious about it, but I was on a career track to be a judge. It was just impossible to give that up. Eventually, I realized I could trust the sitters and my worry diminished. Then I realized how much freedom it gave me. I had found a way to work *and* be a mom."

Bertha, a successful marketing executive, is very clear about her values. "I have accepted the fact that I'm not cut-out to be a full-time mom," she says. "It comes down to knowing yourself." But the opinions of other people—who criticize her behind her back, judge her choices and make off-handed remarks—can still make her feel guilty.

For a woman who has lived her life on a career track, this kind of critical judgment can be unexpectedly jarring and may prey on her own nagging inner feelings. "Before motherhood," one working mother says, "my hard work brought me recognition, approval and privilege, and it seemed to cost me relatively little—a night's sleep, a missed meal, a momentary misunderstanding." Now, the cost in guilt alone is much higher.

For Donna, however, the trade-off is worth it. If she feels a twinge of guilt about working, she takes it in stride. "The truth is," she admits, "by Sunday night I am *kid-ded* to death. When Monday comes around, it's a relief. I find I need the respect of my peers to maintain my sense of self-esteem as a functioning adult.

I love the challenge and the power involved in such a demanding job. Even if I could afford it, I wouldn't give it up."

* * *

For Your Kid

"Just because you don't work, it doesn't mean you're a better mother. My daughter has a much richer life than the kids with moms who stay at home all day."

— Susan

When Susan grew up, she identified more with her active, career-oriented father than with her stay-at-home mother. Her vibrant energy and curiosity drew her toward the enticing world of possibilities. She wanted kids, but never had any intention of giving them the short-shrift by staying home.

Susan takes her daughter on her business trips around the world. She is able to teach her about travel and expose her to new people and places. "Kids are not harmed by moms working," Susan says. "Absolutely not. If anything, my daughter is more mature than other kids. In the end, she'll have more options for her own life."

With the idea that new experiences help make kids more flexible and open-minded, many working moms welcome their kids into their working world. Pat, who works as a bookkeeper at her husband's law firm, has even let her sons start their own business venture on the premises: they own the vending machines in the law suite's lounge. "It teaches them how to manage money and gives them a sense of responsibility," Pat says. She lets them spend half of their profits any way they please, but they must save the other half—and preferably invest it with their father's help.

"I like the idea that in school, afterschool activities and daycare my son can expand his world," Wanda says. "If he stayed home with me all the time, he wouldn't have the same encouragement to expand his social skills and build his own strong network of friends."

Because of her perspective, Wanda has never felt guilty about working. Like Susan, she felt she was giving her son an advantage.

* * *

For Your Relationship

"Now that my son is a teenager, it's important that I work. For one thing, it would be harder for me to let go of him if my whole world revolved around him. This way, he doesn't have to worry about my being there to check on him after school. It gives him the freedom he needs. And it helps our relationship. We'd be fighting more now if I were home."

— Kirstie

While connection with your kid is important, keeping a reasonable distance is equally essential. Kirstie knows that if she were home, she would automatically ask questions that could easily make her sensitive, teenage son feel she was too invasive. By wisely keeping a safe distance, she has made both of their lives work better and has improved their relationship at the same time.

"If I don't get away from the kids sometime, I start to feel frustrated," Donna admits. "Our whole interaction goes more smoothly if I can get away to work. I may be tired but, because I've been away, I'm less likely to snap at them when they cry or whine. I think I'm a better mom because I work."

It's not uncommon to hear mothers say they need time away from their kids, though many feel too guilty to admit it. Keep in mind that it is not a reflection of your love, but a normal human reaction to overload that makes you crave a little breathing room.

✳ ✳ ✳

ABOUT MEETING ALL YOUR KID'S NEEDS

Sickness

"I wonder if I had stayed home with Ben, if he would have a different personality. He's anorexic and seeing a therapist. I think friendships and regular, healthy eating habits were lacking when he was younger. If I had been there, it would have been different..."

—Sally

What mom does not believe, instinctively, that her kids are better off when she's around? Dr. Paula Kaplan, quoted on radio, has pointed out that moms commonly miss work to take their kids to a doctor, even if her husband could do it. Women want to be there, to intervene, to know what's going on, to lend their motherly support. It is the essence of motherhood.

One mother put it simply: "I think my kids recover sooner with me." When work kept her from giving her kids that extra boost, it was easy to feel guilty.

✳ ✳ ✳

Attention

"One of the things I remember most about my years in elementary school was the way my mom was always waiting to take my books and ask me how things went. My older brother hadn't gotten home yet and my dad was still at work and that little bit of extra attention meant so much to me. I want to be there like that for my kids."

— Marta

Each of us has had special experiences we would like to pass on to our kids. Whether it means buying your daughter a copy of *The Secret Garden* or teaching your son to ride a pony, the desire to share an experience is a powerful one. But it is hard to predict what a child will remember.

While her son, Alex, was very young, Georgia worked full-time putting herself through college. Although she knew that meeting her own needs and improving their lives would be valuable to him in the long run, she felt an ever-present backdrop of guilt during those years. When her boy woke up at 3:00 a.m. and crawled onto her lap while she studied, his need to be with her brought tears to her eyes. "I'm not there enough while he's awake," she thought, rocking him to sleep as she read textbooks over his shoulders.

To her surprise, when Georgia finished her degree and had more time to spend with him, Alex bemoaned the loss of their early morning closeness. Despite his mother's feelings of guilt, it was a memory he treasured.

✳ ✳ ✳

Understanding

"Who will be there for Jenny if something is bothering her—if someone has hurt her feelings, if she needs advice or empathy—and I'm at work? Maybe she'll come to me later. But what if the moment passes and I'm not there?"

— Adrienne

As a loving, attentive mom, Adrienne wants to give the best of herself to Jenny, to meet her every need, to be there for her every hour of the day. It may not be realistic—whether Bridget is working or not—but the impulse is strong: "If she needs me, I want to be there."

Yet that same impulse, when charged with guilt, can place unhealthy demands on the child. A mom with a worried, anxious style can make a child feel obliged to be needy. A mom who yearns to be a confidant can become more of a friend than a parent to her child. A healthy fluctuation between closeness and distance, confidence and reticence at different stages of the child's growth—and *different days of the week*—is better for both mother and child.

＊　＊　＊

Emergencies

"I know they'll call me at work if anything happens. But I worried about it so much once the twins were in school that I got a beeper and I timed the drive from my office to the school — 15 minutes on a good day, but I could do it in 10!"

—Janice

A mom's natural concern for her child's safety is heightened when she has to be away at work. Perhaps she feels uncomfortable with the distance from home to work or daycare to work, imagining a catastrophe in which 15 minutes—or even 10 minutes—may not be enough to get there.

"After my kids were born, I went back to work," Dodi says. "They were in a good daycare. I knew they were OK. But when I left them every day, I had this awful feeling that I was forgetting something."

A working mom may not worry at all when her child goes off to camp or spends the night at a slumber party. Conversely, the idea of leaving her daughter with a series of caretakers—from school teachers to music teachers to daycare personnel—while she is at work, makes her feel inexplicably guilty.

"The thing is," Anne told me, "I know no one else cares about him like I do. So how can they take care of him as well I can?"

✳ ✳ ✳

Support

"When I'm home, I try to give Craig all the support I can. I spend time with him and take an interest in his activities. But I worry that it's not enough."

—Bertha

Inevitably, a working mom must face the moment when her kid really needs a hug, but she hasn't gotten home yet. She knows she cannot possibly be there all the time and that when her child learns to tolerate these uncomfortable moments it will actually help her child prepare for some of the unpleasant knocks of life. But that knowledge doesn't always make it easier to face. If she could be there, she would. Knowing it herself and helping her child to understand this can go a long way to alleviating her feelings of regret and guilt.

✳ ✳ ✳

ABOUT STRUGGLING TO MAKE ENDS MEET

"I always expected to have to work. I grew up in a family where both my mother and my father worked. But I don't ever remember feeling they were worried about paying the bills or putting food on the table. Living on just my income, it's really hard to

give my kids the life that they should have. Some nights it keeps me awake, just thinking about it."

—Susan

Statistics show that 20-30 years ago when many of us were growing up, the economy in America allowed parents to buy houses and provide for their kids with unprecedented ease. Those of us who grew up in that era considered it the norm. Our grandparents however, found it harder to make ends meet, as had their grandparents before them.

Today, working moms in single-income families, where their child's father is absent or not working, find it especially hard to pay the bills, build a life for their families and plan for the future. Bearing full financial responsibility for the family can be a heavy burden. Worries over money have kept many moms awake at night. But the degree of guilt they feel about their struggle is often measured by their expectations.

"My mom was always home," Anita explains. "I never wondered how she could manage. I never had to think about it. It made me feel safe. I worry that my son won't have the same sense of security that I did."

❋ ❋ ❋
ABOUT BEING A SINGLE MOM

"I never planned to be a single mom! When I got pregnant, things were going well. John and I were saving to buy a house before Shawn reached school age. Within two years, the marriage was over. I knew it would be harder to be a single mom — but I had no idea!"

—Blaire

Today's families are a mixed bunch. Friends, relatives, professionals, acquaintances and coworkers regularly fill the roles that used to be held only by extended families. Nagged by guilt, single moms look for father figures for their kids wherever they can find them.

According to recent studies, two parent-figures are better for a child than one. But the gender of those parental figures seems to be irrelevant. A devoted aunt or supportive friend standing in place of a parent can offer the child a second, benevolent authority figure. The good news is that a single mom has more options for her child than were previously realized. By seeing those caretakers as essential participants in her child's development, a working mom can genuinely share the complicated task of providing for her child's needs.

❋ ❋ ❋

ABOUT WHAT YOUR KID IS BEING TAUGHT

"We started in a daycare run by a really nice woman who had a good history with kids. But then Jim and I noticed Josh repeating certain prayers over dinner and realized that this woman was instilling her religious beliefs in him. Now we use a live-in with no particular religion. She's more expensive, but we feel we have a little more control over what our son learns and I feel less guilty, knowing that out values are less threatened."

—Audrey

Not just any set of values will do. You want your kid to share your own values and beliefs, if at all possible. Mostly, because you feel *your* values are important; also you want to pass part of your experience on to the next generation, leaving something of yourself behind. Of course, even kids raised at home by their own moms don't always share their parents' views, but the idea of a school or daycare or caretaker imparting values different from yours to your child while you are at work is not only irksome, but alarming.

In the above example, when they discovered an influence they didn't like, Audrey and Jim did what they could to change it. Though they couldn't control every stimulus in Josh's life, the daycare was one adjustment they could make. Hopefully, the live-in had values closer to their own.

It is not uncommon for moms to feel guilty that they have limited control over the values and ideals their children are being taught outside the home. But working tends to magnify these feelings. The uncertainty distresses them. Often they find — as Anne and Jim did — that guilt can lead to positive solutions they would never have found before. The truth is, *guilt* can be *good*.

There is no such thing as a non-working mother.

—*Hester Mundis*

CHAPTER 3

GUILT IS LIKE
A HOT POTATO

guilt \'gilt\ n 1 : *painful feeling of self-reproach resulting from the belief that one has done something wrong or immoral* 2 : *feelings of culpability esp. for imagined offenses or from a sense of inadequacy.*

—*Webster's Dictionary*

From the moment she woke up on Friday, Paula felt in the pit of her stomach a queasy kind of restlessness that made her wince. Last night, things hadn't gone the way she'd planned. After working grueling overtime to get an urgent project out the door, she'd rushed home, slapped some dinner together for the kids, snapped at Jodi when she spilled her Pepsi on the rug and had little patience left to help them with their homework. When she opened her eyes this morning, she wondered: Had she even remembered to kiss them goodnight?

A horrible evening. But, fending off exhaustion, Paula resolved to make it up to them this morning. The problem was, Jodi wasn't speaking to her; Christy kept whimpering and crawling back into bed; and every time she turned her back, Jack started playing

playing Nintendo instead of getting dressed. Most of this was par for the course, but Paula couldn't help thinking that her mood last night had set the tone for the day.

Just as she was starting to feel guilty, the microwave frizzed out, knocking out the power in the house. Reminding Jack again to get ready for school, she headed outside to flip the breaker switch. Her mind was reeling. In the next 30 minutes, she needed to make them something else for breakfast, blow dry her hair, reset all the clocks, reconnect with Jodi, rearrange the paperwork from last night in her briefcase, help Jack and Christy dress and somehow get everyone out the door.

In her heart, she knew that her kids needed special attention this morning as an antidote to her briskness. On top of this, she needed to review her notes for this morning's meeting as well. One thing after another, all morning long, made her feel guilty. But she didn't have time to deal with it now. She just kept tossing her guilt from hand to hand, like the proverbial hot potato.

WHAT DO YOU FEEL?

With all of the things you have to juggle as a working mom, it's easy to rush through the day without ever stopping to notice what you're feeling underneath. One feeling shifts into another and is replaced or pushed aside. You don't have time to deal with it now, so you move on. But bit by bit, you can start to feel overwhelmed.

In my practice, working moms sometimes come through the door feeling so overwhelmed, they aren't even sure what their feelings are. They don't walk in and say, "The guilt is killing me!" Most of the time, they only know they have too much to do and not enough hours in the day to do it. They feel lost and inadequate, in need of help. Their suffering has gone underground, while they cope with everybody else's needs.

What we often find, after careful attention to *their feelings*, is that the guilt is sapping their energy at every step along the way. In our example above, not only did Paula heap guilt upon herself before she even got out of bed, but her kids, trying to meet their own needs, were doing everything to compound her feeling of guilt. Jodi's sullen looks, Christy's whining, and Jack's dogged Nintendo playing, all made her feel more guilty.

When guilt takes over like this, it can deplete us, leaving us exhausted and discouraged. Many emotions such as anxiety, fear, and despair fall into this category. Other feelings — happiness, enthusiasm, surprise — invigorate us and make life more enjoyable. By identifying what we are feeling, we take the first step toward making the best use of every feeling, instead of being overwhelmed.

*   *   *

FEELINGS

The strange thing about some feelings is that you can have them over and over without knowing what they are. "Oh, there it is again!" you say, when you feel that ache in the pit of your stomach and you know it isn't something you ate. Here is a partial list of names for feelings to help you identify those that you often cast aside. Circle the ones that you often feel:

hysterical	*mischievous*	*puzzled*
idiotic	*miserable*	*regretful*
indifferent	*negative*	*relieved*
innocent	*obstinate*	*sad*
interested	*optimistic*	*sheepish*
jealous	*pained*	*shocked*
lonely	*paranoid*	*sympathetic*
lovestruck	*perplexed*	*undecided*
mediatative	*prudish*	*withdrawn*

✽ ✽ ✽

HOW DO YOU EXPRESS YOUR GUILT?

Everyone has her own style of expression and her own Achilles' heel. One woman, who grew up in a family of whiners, may never feel guilty for an instant if her daughter whines. Another woman, happy with a life filled with activity and bustle, may never stop to wonder if the pace is too brisk for her kids.

In Chapter 1, we looked at the ways our family helped to shape our own values and standards as a parent. Those early experiences can help determine what gives us satisfaction as well as what brings pain or guilt. We do, however, have the opportuity and the responsiblity to change if need be.

Now, we'll look at how guilt is expressed.

Actually, there are many modes and most of us use one or all of them at various times. The important thing is to first identify these feelings and keep them under control so they don't negatively affect the different aspects of your life.

Three of the most conspicuous ways guilt is expressed is through our:

❀ body

❀ mind

❀ actions

* * *

The Body

"When Bryan was little, I was working a lot of overtime — 16-20 hours a day—and I was having migraines. Sometimes they would get so bad that I had to call the sitter to take him on Saturday, while I stayed in bed. I couldn't even see him on my one day off!"

—Darla

As guilt builds up inside us, it can manifest itself through feelings of anxiety, exhaustion and sickness.

When your little boy grabs onto your leg and asks, "Mommy, why do you have to go to work?" you know right away what that twist in your stomach means. But other signs are not as easy to interpret.

One mother recently came into my office complaining of fatigue. Lately, she had begun asking her husband to put the kids to bed so she could go to sleep early. She found herself sleeping 9-10 hours a night, yet she always felt wiped out in the morning. She took vitamins, went to the doctor, improved her diet. Nothing seemed to work.

A look at her list of activities showed that what she accomplished every day would run circles around Superman, but she was convinced there was more to it than that. In our subsequent sessions, I suggested some deep relaxation techniques that would take her no more than 5-10 minutes. Gradually, we began to notice the nagging signs of guilt beneath her symptoms of fatigue. Yes, her body was tired and constantly on-the-go. But guilt had been nipping at her heels every day, zapping her energy. When she paused to notice it, she said she could even feel it in her bones!

* * *

THE BODY LANGUAGE OF GUILT

What does guilt feel like? Follow these steps to explore the language of guilt in your body:

❁ *Think of something you feel guilty about.*

❁ *Where do you feel the guilt in your body? In your stomach? In your head?*

❁ *In your neck? In your back?*

❁ *Describe the sensation. Picture it. Make a visual description.*

❁ *If that part of your body could speak, what would it say?*

❁ *Have a conversation with that part of your body—say it out loud, think it in your head or write the conversation in your journal. What does it want you to know?*

* * *

The Mind

"I guess I wasn't aware of it at first, but there is this little voice in my head that harps at me all day long—saying things I would NEVER let anyone else say to me! It seems determined to make me feel bad about whatever I do."

—Janet

Often, long before guilt seeps into your body with symptoms ranging from fatigue to even more serious illnesses, you become aware of it as a little voice in your head.

It's more than likely that something will happen *every day* that doesn't live up to what you planned. What you tell yourself about this disappointment will determine whether you see it as simply water off a duck's back or the final straw.

Here's a quick and easy way to make things 10 times worse. Think of something that you want to do that didn't work out before. You would hear these phrases over and over again:

"It's all my fault."

"I'll never be able to do it."

"How could I possibly think I'd succeed?"

Or you might start citing examples from your life—reinterpreting everything to prove your point: "I'm a schmuck." or "I'm so stupid." Therapists refer to this as "global thinking" because one simple little thing gets blown up until it seems as big as the planet itself.

It seems silly when you see it in writing. Yet it can go on in our heads for days—this nasty little voice in the background, undermining everything we do and making us feel guilty.

The saying "It's all in your head" comes from just this type of situation. Often, 90 percent of the problem can be eliminated by tossing a lasso around this kind of negative self-talk, grabbing its horns and pulling it to the ground. Now you can begin to put things in perspective. In your heart, you know that "everything" is not your fault. How could it be? So many other people and unforeseeable events are involved. It may **feel** like everything is your fault, when you are overwhelmed by guilt, but it is not and you know better. Now your rational mind is taking charge and the emotion of guilt becomes the positive force that got you there.

The trick is to remind yourself of that at just the right moment. Be on the alert for negative, global messages. The moment you start to think: "See, it's all your fault!" That's the time to intervene. You can actually stop that thought with a positive affirmation. Try one of these examples:

- ❀ "I know I feel like everything is my fault right now, but I know I am only partly responsible."

- ❀ "Sometimes I think I am a schmuck, but the truth is I am a wonderful, loving mother who is doing her best."

- ❀ "I am pretty discouraged but I will succeed in the long run. I've done it before."

- ❀ "I am afraid I will not be able to do this, but I can do it —either by myself or with the support of my family and friends."

A good way to tell whether this technique is working for you is to notice your actions. Have you stopped your negative thoughts? Do you know better than to take global thinking seriously? Or has the guilt slipped from your thoughts to your behavior?

✳ ✳ ✳

THE VOICE OF GUILT

What does guilt sound like inside your head? Start to listen for destructive messages. Working moms are especially vulnerable to messages like these:

"You weren't cut out to be a mother."

"The daycare worker is a better parent than you are."

"How can you be so insensitive?"

"You're ruining your child."

"You'll never be as good at this as your mother."

or "You're as bad at this as your mother."

"How can you be so selfish?"

Now list five self-talk messages that make you feel guilty and inadequate. Next time you hear them, stop to notice. Then, insert a positive message before this negative message becomes "global." Remember: just because you hear them, doesn't mean they're true.

1._____

2._____

3. _____

4._____

5. _____

* * *

Your Actions

"Two months after I had John Paul, I didn't want to go back to work. He was so tiny! It was especially hard to turn him over to someone else when I was still nursing. For the first few weeks back at work, I cried every morning. Luckily, my co-workers had kids. They knew what I was going through."

—Serena

Sadness, disappointment, guilt and longing were all mixed together in Serena's tears. Whether she acknowledged each of these emotions to herself or not, she was well-aware of being overcome by her emotions. Crying is like a flashing red light. Not all expressions of feelings are so clear.

If we weren't clever, inventive beings, we wouldn't have survived the stresses of our lives for as long as we have. Over the years, we have each learned ways to act on instinct and quickly avoid the pangs of guilt. We do this so fast, we don't realize it. It is a valuable, though often expensive, means of coping. Great in a crisis, but a dangerous, ineffective habit.

A careful look at our behavior can show us when guilt may be at work. Pay close attention to these reactions. You may not take the time to notice, but your actions mirror your emotions. They can be a signpost to indicate an underlying feeling of guilt.

* * *

Avoiding

One way of dealing with a situation that makes you feel guilty is to avoid it. A working mom's life is filled with so many activities that it's easy to tell yourself you're not really avoiding something —you're just too busy to do it.

In the back of her mind, Carol knew that taking on a new client at work would make her feel guilty about the loss of time with her kids. But the thought of losing such an important client made her feel even worse. Her shoulders tensed-up when she accepted the client. She even caught herself scowling just a bit. But instead of finding an acceptable compromise or weighing the pros and cons of her decision, she told herself the guilt wouldn't bother her—if she didn't think about it.

✳ ✳ ✳

Defending

If the self-talk in your head is constantly criticizing and tearing you down, it's bound to make you irritable. Over time, the working moms who listen day after day to that voice repeating, "You're not a good enough mother. You're doing it all wrong." can begin to feel defensive. They don't want to let it get them down or make them sink into a slump of depression, so they try to shut their feelings off. Instead of countering these messages with positive thoughts that tell their guilt: "I hear you, but I don't agree with what you're saying," they just stop listening.

For Marianne, it was not just the voice in her head, but that of her mother-in-law as well. If Marianne had to work on a weekend or serve the kids TV dinners or anything else her mother-in-law disapproved of, she heard about it. Even worse, Marianne's sisters didn't work and set themselves up as "model" mothers, devoting their lives to their kids. There were unspoken feelings of guilt that she too should be home with her kids. Marianne didn't feel that she could go to them for help because she had to prove that she could handle work and childcare on her own. Gradually, she became so protective of her mothering skills that when one sister offered to do the baby-sitting she so desperately needed, she heard it as a criticism and reacted with anger.

* * *

Overcompensating

It's natural to want to spend more time with your kids at night when you haven't seen them all day or to do something special to make up for not being there. And when guilt takes over, many working moms develop a parenting style that is designed to compensate for their guilt. Much like a divorced parent who only has timesharing weekends and makes every weekend a holiday, they indulge their kids—showering them with gifts, putting their kids' desires before everything else—in a way that sends the wrong message to the kids and reinforces their own guilt.

Betty found herself letting the kids stay up past their bedtime to watch TV on the nights she came home late. Not only did she enjoy having a few more hours to spend with them, but it defused her guilt. In the end, her kids didn't know what to expect from her. With inconsistent boundaries, she hadn't let them know the rules. And her kids eventually learned to play on her feelings of guilt in order to stay up late or watch another hour of TV.

* * *

Losing control

Like crying, losing control is a flashing light that's hard to ignore. Any time emotions are allowed to build up without acknowledgment, there is an outburst in the making. It often occurs in surprising ways.

"If I keep pushing myself all week, without being aware of what's going on inside me," Suzanna says, "my kids start to notice it. Normally, I'm happy and fairly easygoing, but I start to get cranky and less tolerant. If the kids make too much noise or do some of the maddening things kids can do, I just lose it."

✳ ✳ ✳

Somaticizing

Some physicians say that 80-90 percent of our physical ailments are brought about by psychological stress. It's not uncommon to hear holistic practitioners today talk about a "cancer personality," implying that even cancer can be influenced by the way a person deals with anger or other emotions.

Guilt can be one of the most destructive emotions we feel. Because it is traditionally a negative feeling that we turn against ourselves, our bodies have become especially vulnerable to its impact. Ulcers, migraines, nervous disorders and fatigue are only a few of the symptoms that can be caused by guilt — guilt that is seen as negative.

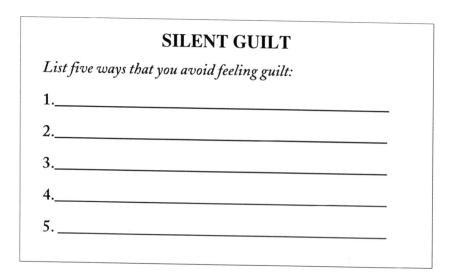

SILENT GUILT

List five ways that you avoid feeling guilt:

1._____

2._____

3._____

4._____

5._____

GUILT'S SECRET ALLY

Quietly biding its time at the heart of guilt is EXPECTATION. Like a secret ally, it supports and encourages guilt. Without it, guilt would not take hold.

Think about it. If you did not expect to be able to meet your children's every need, to answer whenever they called, to be there to cheer their first step, you would not feel guilty when you didn't do it. Doing away with your expectations or your guilt is not the answer. But there is no need to set yourself up for more guilt.

Many times, your expectations were handed down to you from your family. The things your own mom did or didn't do made up part of your expectations. But, ironically, the strongest expectations can come from things your parents *never* did. "A good mother plays with her kids every day," your own mom may have said. You may know for a fact that she never took time to play with you, but you still grew up thinking that "a good mother plays with her kids every day." It doesn't matter if anyone did it or not, the myth became an expectation.

Take a look at the expectations that lead to your feeling of guilt. Ask yourself where they came from. Are they realistic? Are they based on someone else's values or your own? Guilt is only useful when it comes from expectations you believe in. And then — in the right doses — it can be one of the most valuable advisors, keeping you on track like nothing else can!

✳ ✳ ✳

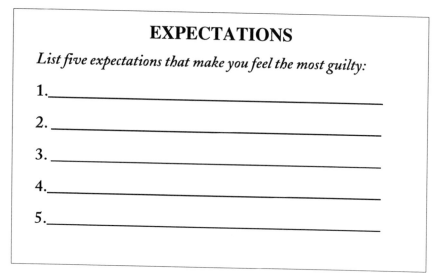

EXPECTATIONS

List five expectations that make you feel the most guilty:

1._____

2. _____

3. _____

4._____

5._____

AFFIRMATIONS FOR EXPECTATIONS

✿ *Yes! It is okay to be a working mother!*

✿ *My child's love for me will not be replaced by another caregiver.*

✿ *No! I will not do my children irreparable harm by working.*

✿ *No! I do not have to jeopardize my career.*

✿ *Yes! I do not have to be a perfect Mom.*

CHAPTER 4

HOW MUCH GUILT IS GOOD?

*If you don't feel guilty, you never change anything. I don't like
feeling guilty, but it works.*

—*Deborah*

GUILT IDENTIFIED

Awareness of your guilt is the first step in putting it to good
use. But if you are like most working moms, you're so busy
that you don't usually take time to explore what you're feeling. If
someone asks: "How do you feel?" you're likely to wonder: "Who
has time to notice?"

You may be well aware that how you feel — how you *experience*
life—is important in the long run. But the most urgent thing
today is to get the chicken defrosted for dinner, pick-up your
daughter from soccer practice, and stop by the dry cleaners. If
you're lucky, you'll get home in time to make dinner, balance your
checkbook, work on tomorrow's presentation for a new client and
get everyone cleaned-up and into bed before midnight. "How do

you feel?" may be a good question, but it is one that working moms are usually too busy to answer.

The trouble is, waiting until you have time to notice your feelings is like waiting until you have a little extra money. Maybe it will happen on its own, but don't hold your breath. Chances are, you will have to *make it* happen.

It may help to realize that checking in with yourself on a regular basis is one of the most vital keys to keeping your sanity. You need to take your feelings into account for your *emotional* well being as much as you need food and drink for *physical* well being. As a bonus, tending to your feelings will lend you such peace of mind that, in the long run, your loved ones will thank you for the serenity it brings to the family as a whole.

Approach your feelings as you would approach someone you love—with empathy, respect and kindness, ready to accept and forgive, to offer your support. Move through each of the steps below:

❁ Stop to Listen

You start by stopping.

That still, small voice inside you isn't going to shout over the dishwasher and a room full of noisy kids. Make the time and space to hear it, just for five minutes a day.

"It's kind of weird," said Talia, a busy, working mom, "but the best place for me to be alone is in the bathroom. For a few, sweet moments, no one will bother me there. I used to hang out in the garden on the side of the house, but the kids would track me down. So the bathroom has become a kind of haven. I've even added a small vase of fresh flowers in there to make it more my own."

✽ Stay Open to Whatever You're Feeling

After setting aside some time in a quiet, private place, allow yourself to relax into your feelings. Be sure to give yourself the same consideration you would give someone else. Stay open. For these few moments, let yourself feel whatever you're feeling. No plans. No judgment. No expectations. It's just you, yourself and the four walls. For once, let all of your attention rest on you. Yes, you have permission.

✽ Identify the Feeling

Once you allow yourself a quiet space for your feelings, you will be surprised by what you experience. You may find that your feelings are stronger than you realized or you may become so tense over having repressed your feelings that, once you can relax, you'll discover the tension , which registers physically, was worse than the feeling itself.

The key benefit of identifying and distinguishing feelings is that they become easier to handle. It makes sense, when you think about it. If you handle your feelings one at a time, you know what your are dealing with and you can look for alternative ways to handle them, rather than just letting them build up inside you.

Initially, you may feel a little twinge that tells you, "I feel bad about that. Jimmy deserves more attention, but I don't have time tonight." Believing there's nothing you can do about it now, you push the feeling down and try to put it out of your mind.

Then the next message chimes in, making things worse: "You never have time. You always say you're going to spend more time with him, but you never do. Don't you love him? Isn't Jimmy more important than work?" A simple event (running out of time tonight) becomes a terrible character flaw. If you try to push this feeling aside as well, you're asking for trouble.

The old pressure cooker analogy applies perfectly to feelings. No matter how hot the soup gets inside, there's no danger of explosion when the top is loose. But when you lock down the lid and turn up the flame, the pressure starts to build. Then, once you remove the lid, the soup literally hits the fan!

Stopping to give yourself time for your feelings is an effective way of taking off that lid before the pressure builds up too much. As time goes by, you'll become more aware of your feelings, even when they simmer and long before they start to boil.

Be on the look out for messages in your head that make things worse than they really are. Watch out for phrases like: "You always..." "You never..." and "Don't you care?"

Take the time to explore these messages of guilt to find out what *kind* of guilt you're feeling. Is it meant to help you to grow emotionally or is it just trying to make you miserable? Is it putting things in a bigger perspective or in a harsh, unflattering light? What purpose does your guilt serve?

❋ ❋ ❋

Know You Can Handle Guilt

It's not uncommon for working moms to use the hustle and bustle of their lives to distance them from their feelings. They are genuinely busy, but feeling they have to "do it all" may be a shield, protecting them from their feelings. Part of the fear is that if they *feel* their feelings they will have to either act on them or extinguish them. They are afraid they will be overwhelmed. Many feel the only safe way to cope with guilt is to deny it. "I don't feel guilty," Debbie told me. "It's a luxury I can't afford. It doesn't do any good."

The truth is, knowing you can handle feelings of guilt—and recognize them—will make you feel empowered. In her book *Feel the Fear and Do It Anyway,* Susan Jeffers,Ph.D. insists that "at the bottom of every one of your fears is simply the fear that you can't handle it." If you let that fear stop you, you'll never discover the relief of knowing that whatever you are feeling —guilt, anger, frustration, sadness—it is something you *can* handle!

* * *

GETTING TO THE GUILT OF THE MATTER

Once you have identified a feeling as guilt, find out what kind of guilt it is. Is it guilt that scolds or guilt that coaches?

Guilt that Scolds has the shrill voice of a nagging parent. It is rude, bad tempered and unforgiving. Usually, it repeats itself and the message is the same. Day after day, it freely accuses you of not living up to its own unrealistic expectations.

In fact, you may find that you don't even share the same values as that scolding voice! "When I snapped at Sam last week, I felt sorry and apologized," Laila admitted. "But then that voice started in: 'What kind of mother would snap at her kid? He's going to grow up thinking you're a shrew!'"

When you take the time to really listen to the Guilt that Scolds, one thing becomes immediately clear: it just wants to make you feel bad; it isn't trying to help.

Guilt that Coaches is very different. It may be just as tenacious and tug on your stomach with a similar sense of dread, but it is good intentioned. In a quiet moment, you might hear it say, "There is something you've forgotten or overlooked."

Guilt itself doesn't offer any suggestions. It just points out, over and over again, that something needs to be fixed. This is the kind of urging you can use. It's a helpful warning, like a flashing light: "Jon needs more attention!" "You've missed a number of deadlines at work!" "I thought you said that you were going to rest!"

Each one, surrounded by her own characteristics (bad tempered, unforgiving/good intentioned, corrective) or even the kind of remarks they might make ("There you go again!"/"Don't forget!")

GO WITH YOUR GUILT

Once you've identified your feeling as guilt, the next step is to spend a little time getting to understand it. It may seem like you already know this unpleasant feeling only too well! But there is an enormous difference between letting guilt harp at you all day or really stopping to listen to its message. It is like vaguely hearing someone speak behind you, then turning around to look him in the eye. If you look at him, you know a lot more about what he's saying. You've given him your full attention. Only if you let guilt have your attention now and then, will you alleviate it.

Every time you spend 5 minutes paying attention to guilt, you relieve yourself of 15 minutes of stress. The relief is amplified. On the other hand, if you avoid guilt and involve yourself in activities to take your mind off it, it may take twice as long to fix later on.

Set aside some time every day. Some working moms find a moment early in the morning. Others like to take part of their lunch hour at work to find a private place. Experiment with different times and places to find what's best for you. "I know there are things I feel guilty about," Sophia says. "When I start to get that feeling, I try to relax and let it in. For me, guilt is a positive motivator."

The important thing is to find a way to let guilt help you, to work with it, get to know it and let it know you're listening. You'll be surprised by the results.

FOCUS EXERCISE

TIME: 5 minutes

✿ *Close your eyes and sit quietly. Notice how your entire body feels. Are you holding your breath or breathing evenly?*

✿ *Slowing your breathing down and letting go of any thoughts you may have, start to breath in ... and ... out ... and ... in ... and ... out. Focus on how your body feels. Begin by noticing just your feet and nothing else. Notice the feeling in the bottom of your feet—in your toes, you arches, your heels.*

✿ *Now, as you take a deep breath, tense or squeeze the muscles in your feet and hold them as tight as you can ... now gradually release the tension in your muscles as you breathe out. Continue to breath, calmly and softly.*

✿ *Now focus your attention on your legs and nothing else. Notice how they feel. As you breathe in deeply, squeeze the muscles in your calves, your knees, your thighs and hold these muscles tight ... then release the tension in your legs as you breathe out.*

✿ *Continue this process with your bottom and pelvis area; up through your arms, chest, shoulders and back area; through your neck and face; and finally, through your arms and hands.*

✿ *Continue to breathe deeply. Focus on each group of muscles individually. Hold these muscles tightly for about 10 seconds and then gradually relax them. When you have completed all of these areas, count to 3 and slowly open your eyes.*

As you focus your attention on breathing in deeply, on tightening and relaxing each muscle group and on each part of the body, you are learning to focus your attention on what is before you. You become less distracted, more centered and calm. You are now closer to your true feelings and closer to yourself.

* * *

Express Yourself

All of us have different ways of discovering our feelings and expressing them. Just as we use our memory to learn about others, in the same way we can discover and learn about ourselves. For some of us, it's easier to remember what someone says if we write it down. For other people, hearing words make more of an impression. For still others, movement or images have the strongest impact. Because we experience the world through all of our senses, we can make use of any of them. But the chances are good that you will have a preference.

As you express your feelings of guilt, try each of the approaches below to see which one suits you best. You may choose to switch between them, use all of them, or settle on a favorite. Let yourself explore.

* * *

Writing

"Journaling" has become a popular American pastime. Bookstores have whole sections devoted to beautiful fabric or leather-covered blank books for those who have discovered the advantages of writing down their thoughts. The truth is, any old notebook or scrap of paper will do. But by choosing a book that is particularly appealing and special to you, you can remind yourself that "Yes, this is important to me. What I write in this book has value. And my feelings are vital to me and my well being."

Follow one or all of the methods for:

MAPPING OUT YOUR GUILT

1. Say the word "guilt" aloud. For 5 minutes, write down everything that comes into your mind. You can make a list or scatter words and phrases all over the page. Now look carefully at what you've written. Circle words that are similar. Is there a general theme in these words? How much space does guilt take up in your life? When your 5 minutes are up, leave this page. But go back to it later for a fresh look. Add to it if you like.

2. Keep a running list throughout the day. Every time you notice a twinge of guilt, jot down a word or phrase that will remind you of it. At the end of the day, take an honest look at your list. How many times did you feel guilty today? 5 times? 10 times? too many times to write down? Now look at the messages connected with your guilt. Did it scold or coach you?

3. What does the Guilt that Scolds say to you? Write down its complaints. How many of them are based on what someone else has said or what they think you should be doing?

4. What does the Guilt that Coaches say to you? How is it encouraging you to change? What can you do to make the best use of its advice? How will you take charge of this?

---

* * *

Imaging

As tempting as it may be, it's probably best not to try this one at work! Anyone who *has* tried imaging will tell you how valuable it is to imagine your feeling as a character and hold a conversation with it. For one thing, it gives you a little distance. It is removed from you; it becomes a separate entity you can see.

The trick is to let your imagination run free. Visualize your guilt in any form that comes to mind. Treat that image with respect. It is like a leprechaun and will quickly vanish if you don't acknowledge its reality.

Novelists and playwrights have always said that once they imagine a character, it takes on a life of its own. Often they're surprised by the things the character says or refuses to say! After you try this exercise, you'll know what they mean.

LET'S TALK

Pick a place for your guilt to sit. You can pull up an empty chair or find a spot at the foot of the bed. Just make sure it's the same place every time.

You may want to use the Focusing Exercise to feel relaxed enough to home in on the feeling. Once you have a clear sense of what your guilt feels like, let it sit in the empty chair or whatever place you've made for it.

Now you're ready to start the interaction. You can chat, argue, explain, bargain—anything at all. Just start talking. Then listen to what your guilt has to say. Here are a few questions to ask your guilt that may help to get things going:

✿ *What bothers you so much?*

✿ *What do you want from me?*

✿ *What can I do to help?*

✿ *What is the best way to tackle this problem?*

✿ *What will you do to help?*

✿ *What do we do next?*

Marla has two kids in grade school and works from 8 a.m. to 4 p.m. as a paralegal in a law firm. Normally, she doesn't indulge in flights of fancy. She doesn't have time! But when her guilt about leaving her kids in the care of others started to get to her, she decided to try this exercise.

Once the kids were asleep, she sat down on her bed and imagined Guilt sitting on the footboard at the end of her bed. It was like a gargoyle hunching its face over long spindly fingers. It looked fierce at first, but as she started speaking, it seemed to listen up.

MARLA: I notice I've been feeling sad and worn out the past few days. Is that because of you?

GUILT (smiling):Yes.

MARLA: What is it? Are you just trying to make me feel bad or did you have something to say?

GUILT: I keep telling you to spend more time with the kids. Can't you see how they're suffering? They need more time with you.

MARLA: I know they need more time with me and I'm working on it. In two weeks, I'm going to start leaving work at 3:00. Things will be better then. None of us are happy with the way it is now, but I wouldn't say they're "suffering."

GUILT: Well, maybe not "suffering"... but it could be better.

MARLA: True. But I'm on it. You let me know if you're worried about anything else, but don't keep making me feel bad about this. Deal?

GUILT: Deal.

✳ ✳ ✳

Drawing

You may want to borrow your kids' crayons here. Find a big tablet of newsprint or some other inexpensive paper and you are ready to begin.

As with the other exercises, allow yourself to focus on the feeling of guilt before you start. Let all other thoughts drift away. Notice what color your guilt is. Now grab that color crayon and start to draw.

How big is it? What kind of expression do you see on its face? You don't have to be an artist to create an impression on the page. Give yourself permission to draw whatever you feel. The point is to make it tangible, to bring it to life.

Once you've drawn your picture, take a close look at it. Turn it sideways. Turn it upside down. You may not be able to put everything you see into words. The colors you've chosen will help convey your emotion. The shape may not look like much of anything, but it will say a lot about your feelings.

However it turns out, you can look at it and say, "This is what my guilt looks like today." Now save it. Put it in a place where you can find it. Strange as it may seem, this drawing will strongly connect with the part of you that feels your guilt. Keep it. Use it to talk to, negotiate with it. Respect it.

You will find that when you take the trouble to pay attention to your guilt in one of these ways, it will gradually become less of an adversary and more of a friend.

Once you've identified your guilt and brought it to life, you are in a strong position. Now that you know what you're dealing with, ask yourself:

❁ Which guilt is helpful, reminding you of something you can change?

❁ Which guilt is not helpful, tormenting you about something you can't change?

It's normal to feel different kinds of guilt about different things. After you have decided which feelings are helpful and which are not, you can decide what to do next. Here are several options.

❋ ❋ ❋

Take Action

"Not having time to clean up the house was really getting to me. I was rushing around in a whirlwind—from home to school to work to school and back—and the house was starting to look like it had been hit by that same whirlwind. A friend suggested that I spend no more than 10 minutes a night picking up. I was surprised at what a difference it made in the house. But the biggest change was in my feelings— what a relief from guilt!"

— Sonja

If you're feeling guilty about something you can change, explore different ways to achieve your goal. Often, friends and relatives can offer good suggestions or pitch in to help. When you're dissatisfied with a lot of things in your life, take them one at a time. It's a good idea to make a list of your goals. Put the most important ones at the top of the list, then make a plan. How are you going to accomplish these goals? What steps can you take today, next week or next month? Who can help you achieve them?

Be on the look-out for sabotage. By expecting things to change immediately or to happen perfectly, you can accidentally booby-trap your goals. When Marge determined to leave work on time every day, so she could spend more time with her son, she ran into obstacles. Her employer was used to getting "just one more" project out the door at 5 p.m. It took her two weeks to work things out. In the meantime, Marge says, "I felt *twice as guilty* as I had before! Not only was I staying late, I was blowing my goal. It took awhile for me to realize that I was still on track. It just took longer than I'd hoped."

As you work your way toward each goal, be sure to acknowledge yourself for the progress you make. If you get dinner on the table on time six out of seven days a week, give yourself credit. Remember, perfection isn't human. It isn't even desirable. In fact, it only serves to intimidate those around you.

❋ ❋ ❋

Call a Truce

"Last Christmas, I decided to take two weeks off. But that meant working overtime for the first part of December to finish the year end reports. I didn't have time to create much Christmas spirit for the kids, but it was the best I could do. Luckily, I make a pact to give myself credit for braving the extra time-off with

less money in order to have time at home. I called a truce on guilt."

— Raylene

Now that you've begun to build a relationship with your guilt, you have bargaining power. It never works to ignore your guilt and shove it out of the way. Stifling those turbulent feelings will send your stress level through the ceiling! But calling a truce is another matter.

At this point, you can speak to your guilt directly and explain the situation. A slight shift in your approach can give you a great deal of relief. Like Rayann, you may find that you can get that nagging voice to lighten up.

* * *

Get Support

"When I get too down on myself, I just call someone—usually another working mom—and spill the beans. It's like saying 'Here's how badly I feel about myself. What do you think?' I'd never make it without such good friends."

— Marta

There is a reason why groups like AA are so popular. The support network they provide is strong, reliable and available almost 24-hours a day. Your own personal support group may not be as accessible but having one to help offset the guilt and manage your life is absolutely vital. "There are so many working moms at my office, that I find work to be a great resource," Kathy says. "We all sit around the table in the lunch room on our breaks and talk about our problems with our kids. Motherhood is like a great club!"

Sometimes all you need is a little understanding. In fact, if the truth be known, it may be all you have time for! The great thing is that, with friends, giving can be just about as good as receiving.

✳ ✳ ✳

Repeat Affirmations

"For me, guilt is like a broken record, playing the same old tune. If I don't counteract it with affirmations, I just hear that nonsense over and over in my head."

— Lilly

The well of blame and accusations runs very deep in some working moms, and can spew out a stream of criticism that's hard to silence. Affirmations can help to override that negative voice. Some people repeat them to themselves. Others paste them to their dashboard, their computer, their bathroom mirror or carry them in their purse. Sometimes they change affirmations every day, go to sleep listening to a tape of them or recite a favorite affirmation like a mantra. You may find even more ways to use them.

✳ ✳ ✳

AFFIRMATIONS FOR MOMS

Here is a sample of some affirmations you may use. Be free to create your own, but be sure to write them down when you do.

❀ *Today I will forgive that I am not the perfect parent*

❀ *Today I am going to feel the fear and do it anyway*

❀ *Today I really will do something for me*

❀ *Today I will say, "No" to something I do not want to do or do not have time for*

Take Time Out

With all the responsibilities she has to handle, a full-time mom can hit overload very easily. Add to that the responsibilities of working and you have a guaranteed *recipe* for stress.

What feels like crushing disappointment, guilt or even heartbreak can sometimes be nothing more than exhaustion. It's hard to remember to take care of yourself, when you're so busy taking care of everyone else. But, as we've always heard, an ounce of prevention is worth a pound of cure. Taking a little time out for yourself everyday is the best way to avoid overload. It doesn't have to be expensive or time consuming. The main thing is so get the most out of it that you can.

STRESS BUSTERS

✿ *Music. Put on the headphones and listen to your favorite music. It's one of the most comforting things you can do.*

✿ *Quiet. The other option is to put on the headphones and listen to nothing. Sometimes nothing's better.*

✿ *Friends. Remember those gossipy, half-hour-long phone calls with a girlfriend? It's like riding a bike—you never forget how to do it.*

✿ *Candlelight. In your room just before bedtime, at dinner or while you're taking a bath, it's both soothing and luxurious.*

✿ *Books. One of the best treats in the world is to immerse yourself in a good book—even just a few pages a night.*

✿ *Sex. You remember sex; it's how everything got started. Not only is it fun, but it's one of the best all-over relaxant you can get.*

✿ *Escape. Ride, walk, run, bike, skate, sail, hike—for 30 minutes or so a day. It clears your mind and gives you new perspective.*

✿ *Laugh. Kids excel at laughter. Let them share it: play with your kids. Listen to a comedian on TV. Read a funny book. And watch the stress disappear.*

✿ *Treats. Sometimes little pleasures are the most refreshing. Save your favorites for those stressed-out afternoons and indulge yourself.*

CHAPTER 5

WORKING MOM 2001

What business needs now is exactly what women are able to provide... and that gives women unique opportunities to assist in the continuing transformation of the workplace by express-ing, not by giving up, their personal values.

—*Sally Helgeson*

From the waitress living on the tips she makes pouring coffee in a diner to the attorney hoping for a percentage of the gross as a partner in her firm, working moms everywhere are reshaping the job market. Women have become a dominant force in the workplace. As a result, their values and concerns have been given increasing priority.

Guilt is among those concerns. When an office is filled with women who feel guilty about working till 6 p.m. when their kids get off at 2 p.m., it's only a matter of time before something starts to shift.

In the past, attending to the needs of working moms was the nice thing to do. Today, corporations everywhere are discovering that it's not just nice—it's the smart thing to do.

By allowing their full-time workers to work part-time hours without giving up benefits, a bank in Memphis recently found that 85 percent of the workers who were planning to quit for family reasons decided to stay. As a result, productivity increased and the bank actually saved money. Not only were their employees happier, but the bank's customers were happier as well. "Now we're all singing off the same page of the hymnal," the manager said.

* * *

ADAPTING YOUR JOB TO YOUR LIFE

Not every employer can be at the cutting edge of change, and some are just paying lip service to change. But many, especially those who have kids of their own, are more willing to listen to and explore new options that will meet their business needs, while improving your contentment on the job. By now, your employer may already be aware that there are many legitimate alternatives to a traditional 9 to 5 job. If some of them appeal to you, go ahead and suggest them! Let's take a look.

* * *

Working with Flextime

"In accounts payable, we always worked twice as hard at the beginning of the month. Then someone came up with the idea of working longer shifts the first half of the month and going home early in the second half. Now I can actually be there when my kids come home from school!"

— Mindy

Even though it's unconventional, flextime often creates a win-win situation for both employees and businesses. At Mindy's company, customer accounts were reconciled twice as fast on the new system. The company was happy and Mindy found that her level of guilt dropped significantly.

The demands of kids make it hard to comply with a predictable schedule at best. Sometimes it's impossible. Because her employer isn't open to the idea of flextime, Deborah has created her own version of flextime with her husband. "We just trade off," she says. "If the kids need to go to the doctor or have an unexpected day off from school, we use up our vacation time and sick leave to be with them. By the end of the year, we usually don't have any paid time off left between us."

❊ ❊ ❊

Working Part-time

"I knew that if I scrimped and saved, I could get by on part-time income until Jessie went to school. But I was always afraid of giving up the insurance. What if one of us got sick?"

— Esther

When insurance premiums are so much higher for individuals than for groups, many working moms can't afford to replace the insurance package provided by their employer. You may be able to buy reasonable insurance on a group plan through your bank, credit union or trade organization. But it is not uncommon for an employer to extend insurance coverage to part-time employees, after a little negotiation.

"Part-time work is perfect for me," Julie says. "I use a babysitter two days a week and take three days off. Raising kids is the hardest thing I've ever done; working is easy. So I need to get away. If I were home more than that, I'd end up fighting with the kids. For two days a week, work is like a haven."

WORKING MOM NEGOTIATES PART-TIME JOB WITH BENEFITS!

When her son, John, was born, Mariah found it hard to leave him in childcare. She had been trying to have a baby for years and now that John had finally been born, she wanted to spend as much time with him as possible. After many late night discussions with her husband, trying to find a way for her to stay home full-time, she realized that they couldn't afford it; she would have to go back to work.

Fortunately, the two attorneys Mariah worked for were family men; one had three sons, the other had just had his first baby. They had both had personal experience of how hard it was to be away from their kids. After she had been back for a couple of weeks, Mariah approached them with a proposal.

First, she pointed out that, because of the computer courses she had taken over the years, she had been finishing their work in four days for quite some time. If they allowed her to take Fridays off, they wouldn't have to pay her for the extra day! "But I'll still need those benefits," she told them. "Medical insurance is more important to me now than ever."

The attorneys agreed that, as long as Mariah was willing to stay late occasionally if need be, she could keep her benefits and work four days a week.

The advent of computers and highly skilled workers has eliminated a lot of time consuming work from full-time jobs. In a job like this, going part-time may give you the extra time you've been craving with your kids.

If taking two days a week off to stay at home with your kids would make the pile of work unbearable for the other three days, you might consider taking one day off yourself and having your spouse or significant other take a day off as well. That way, each of you can work more, but your child will have a parent at home two days a week. Creative compromises are the essence of the solution. Sometimes it takes a little trial-and-error to see which solution works best.

Considering the cost of daycare, working more is not always the most economical solution. "I make good money as an attorney," Debbie says. "But I pay $26,000 a year in childcare. One kid costs $730 a month. I don't know how mothers making less than I do can manage."

For Sophia, the advantages of working full-time aren't worthwhile—either emotionally or financially. "We pay too high a price for the second salary," she complains. "I feel I'm giving up raising my kids to have another income. And the really sad thing is that, after daycare, we're only coming out $400 ahead. It's pathetic. But my kids have a lot more than I did when I grew up—they have a lot of love."

✳ ✳ ✳

Working at Home

"It took a little work to set up a private space where I could work at home, but it was worth it. It doesn't mean I'm always available to spend time with the kids, but I'm there."

— Betsy

Faxes, modems, telephones and open-mindedness have made telecommuting a reality for many working moms. Some go into the office a few days a week. Others work for an employer halfway across the country, whom they have never met face-to-face.

It takes some getting used to. The temptation to putter around the house or sit down in the living room with a toddler and his blocks is much greater when there is a pile of work stacked-up on your desk. Working at home not only takes more discipline, it requires setting firm boundaries.

Even though they are working at home, many moms still have a sitter all day to watch their kids. The most successful moms are able to put all of their attention on work for certain hours of the day, but take occasional breaks to interact with their kids. One mom goes out the front door in the morning, as if she's going to work, and comes back into her office from the side door to *physically* make the transition between roles. When her kids come home in the afternoon, she spends an hour or so with them, helping with their homework, asking about their day. Then when they go outside to play with friends, she gets in a few more hours of work.

It isn't the same as having free time to devote to your kids all day. But with clear-cut boundaries, it can help alleviate the nagging, guilty feeling that you are not home enough for your kids.

❊ ❊ ❊

Working out a Job Share

"When Helen started kindergarten, I wanted to switch to part-time, but I had too much work to do that. Then I met Ellen at the PTA. She had the same skills as I did and was looking for part-time work in the afternoons! We decided to job-share. Next I approached my boss and—with less trouble than I'd expected—sold him on the idea of job sharing."

— Natasha

Short of bumping into the perfect match, like Natalie did, there are other ways of working out a job sharing arrangement. With a little creativity and determination, any one of these might work for you:

- ❀ find someone in your office who wants more work — a part-time worker looking for full-time hours; a full-time worker who could use some extra money;

- ❀ apply for a new position with a partner who wants to job share from the beginning, if your current employer isn't open to the idea;

- ❀ interview prospective job share partners yourself and agree to oversee and train them while they learn the other half of your job.

Keep your mind open to new solutions. Some job shares are divided unevenly in a way that suits everyone concerned. Your dream job may require you to work 4 days a week. A one-day-a-week helper may be all the sharing you need. Two days on with three days off or even five mornings a week may be viable possibilities.

✳ ✳ ✳

JOB SHARE/CHILD SHARING SCHEDULE

Gail and Marianne talked their employer, Kitchenmate, into letting them share a job—at least on a trial basis. Both had preschool kids: Gail's daughter, Annie, was 18 months old and Marianne's son, Tyler, was two.

The plan worked out better than anyone had expected. Not only did the two women work well together but, by baby-sitting for each other on alternate days, they reduced their childcare expenses at the same time. Besides that, if either of them wanted to take a special day off occasionally, they simply worked it out between them. Here's a look at their schedule:

GAIL		MARIANNE	
Monday/Tuesday		**Monday/Tuesday**	
8:30-5.30	work at Kitchenmate	8:30-5.30	stay home with Annie & Taylor
Wednesday		**Wednesday**	
8:30-5.30	work at Kitchenmate	8:30-5.30	stay home with Annie & Taylor
1:00-5:30	stay home with Annie & Taylor	1:00-5:30	work at Kitchenmate
Thursday/Friday		**Thursday/Friday**	
8:30-5.30	stay home with Annie & Taylor	8:30-5.30	work at Kitchenmate

Working for Yourself

"I do work longer hours since I started my pottery business, but I can choose those hours. After giving the kids breakfast and getting them off to school, I make phone calls to clients for a few hours and glaze some pots. When the kids get home around 3:00, I get to spend several hours playing with them and asking about their day. In the evenings, when its cool, I get down to throwing pots in earnest. Instead of working 8 hours a day, it's usually more like 10, but the hours are flexible and I love my work."

— Bonnie

Women today are starting businesses twice as fast as men. Since World War II, the number of working women has increased 200 percent. The chance to work for themselves, make their own decisions about how and when they spend their time, and to have the opportunity to stay in closer touch with their family throughout the day, appeals to many working moms.

Recognizing the increased demand, non-profit organizations specifically designed to help women start their own businesses have sprung up across the country. Their sliding scale-fees and group support make it easier for women to make the transition from employment to self-employment. In addition, new networking organizations around the country allow women to share referrals and commiserate on the daily demands of their lives in a new business.

Whether a new business succeeds depends largely on how much time and preparation its owner has invested. When you think about starting a business, every minute you spend (before you open) looking into the costs, marketing possibilities and requirements for your operation will increase your chances for success.

For all the potential satisfaction of being your own boss, starting a business is not for everyone. New business owners must often live with months of long hours and unstable income. You should be aware that, at least initially, it is more likely that you will have *less time*, not more time, to spend with your kids.

With the right determination and preparation, however, a self-run business can give working moms the freedom and flexibility they need.

Recent studies show that doing work you enjoy is one of the more reliable means of self-expression. Review the list of home business possibilities on the next page, then think of the activities you turn to in your spare time. Can any of these activities be adapted to a self-run business?

HOME BUSINESS POSSIBILITIES

Many homes businesses can be started without much initial investment. When they are built on skills you already have, little additional training may be needed. The home businesses listed here could be started on the side and built up as the business grows. Just remember that a new business takes time. In the short term, it could give you even less time to spend with your kids than you have now, though ultimately, it may provide you with much greater freedom.

PRODUCTS	*SERVICES*
greeting cards	*childcare*
baked goods	*gourmet food delivery*
pottery	*closet re-organization*
personalized gifts	*individualized shopping*
pet accessories	*massage*
baby journals	*house/pet/plant sitting*
painted clothing	*fitness training*
hand-crafted jewelry	*seminars and classes*
computer softwarejob	*placement information*
food photography	*computer programming*

ADAPTING YOUR LIFE TO YOUR JOB

Despite the changing awareness about employee needs, many of the women I surveyed said that their life outside of work was deemed to be irrelevant on the job. Deborah laughs when she explains her predicament, but she is concerned about the problem nonetheless. "Sometimes I have to remind people that I don't have a wife at home," she says. "It's as if they don't approve of my 'other life.'"

* * *

In Stacey's experience, it was not only her employer but her co-workers who held that view.

> "When I had my daughter, I took a few years off from the career track. Instead of supporting me, the other women in the office were disappointed. They had seen me as a trail-blazer, taking the lead in the fast lane. They all had kids and families, but they never talked about it. Your life outside the office was restricted to a family picture on your desk; it was never discussed."
>
> — Stacey

In the middle of an early offer to make her a partner, the attorneys at the law firm found out Stacey was pregnant. Without remark, they offered her an hourly contract instead. "I should not have been surprised," Stacey told me. "Even when my husband was in intensive care, they complained."

After her pregnancy leave, Stacey applied to another firm, hoping that at the new firm, her family life would at least be acknowledged. But there, too, she found she was expected to put work above her family, even on special occasions. When a project kept everyone at the office until early the next morning, Stacey left at midnight. Even though she explained that she was throwing a birthday party for her daughter the next day and had to get home, there was little understanding. "They saw it as a lack of commitment to the job," she explained.

Perhaps the most surprising obstacles arise in companies that have a written policy allowing pregnancy leave. If everyone supports the policy, a pregnant mom knows what to expect. But in some cases, an unspoken policy wins the day.

At Caryn's office, pregnancy leave was supposed to last 8 weeks. But in practice, women who had babies were encouraged to take 1 or 2 weeks off. Afraid that her job would be gone if she didn't hurry back, Caryn returned right away. She had wanted to take six months off. That was out of the question. Eight weeks would have been better, but it was too much of a risk.

Now, of course, with the enactment of the Family Leave Act, Caryn is guaranteed the ability to take pregnancy leave and retain her job, with or without her employer's good will. Bringing widespread attention to the problem by a sweeping public policy such as this is a strong beginning for a future of appropriate job flexibility for working parents.

CHANGES ON THE HORIZON

All indications show that the 21st Century will be bright for women in the workforce. Record numbers of businesses will be owned by women. New styles of management that focus on relationships and communication—skills that women have cultivated in their own lives and bring with them to the office—will make it easier to balance the demands of the work and family. The concerns of a woman's life outside the office will not be regarded as insignificant, but will be seen as a natural part of the day.

John Naisbitt, author of *Megatrends 2000,* predicts that, since more than 75 percent of working women are in their prime child-bearing years, daycare will soon become an employee benefit as commonplace as medical insurance and sick days. Already, many companies offer on-site facilities or childcare vouchers to pay a portion of the costs of childcare. Enterprising businesswomen in metropolitan areas have answered the demand by opening general daycare centers for employees who work in high-rise buildings. Many of these innovations began as solutions to the "problem" of guilt. When it motivates creative action, guilt is an indispensable ally!

CHAPTER 6

AM I RUINING
MY KIDS?

[Our families] can get along with less in terms of glowing
performance if we give them a lot in terms of presence. There's
nothing wrong with an exhausted mother cuddling her child
after a dinner that came out of a can. The cuddle will be remem-
bered. The can will be forgotten.

—*Barbara Cawthorne Crafton*

After talking for most of the session about how hard it was to
juggle parenting with work, Laurie checked the clock in my
office. We were almost out of time. A determined look came over
her face. No more beating around the bush, it seemed to say.
"What I want to know is this," she blurted out, "If I work, am I
ruining my kids?"

Underneath the frustration and anxiety and sheer aggravation
of balancing so many conflicting demands, one of the greatest
concerns of working moms is whether it will have a long-term
impact on the health and well-being of their kids. "I try not to
expose them to my guilt too much," Lynn admits. "But sometimes

I wonder, do I really know them?" In the everyday rush of activities, it's easy to feel you are missing out.

More often than not, these mothers underestimate how much they are accomplishing. Every mom has moments with her kids that she would like to go back and change. Maybe she didn't know any better at the time or maybe her guilt let her know right away that she had made a mistake—but she couldn't go back.

The good news is, you don't have to go back. Believe it or not, there are some things more important for your kids than doing things right every step of the way. It's much healthier and more normal to get off track, to feel guilty and then, correct your course. Think of guilt as a navigational system, much like the ones on airplanes.

Most people aren't aware that an airplane doesn't fly directly from one point to another. Instead, it uses an inertial guidance system to make constant adjustments so that the plane will arrive within five minutes of the estimated arrival time. Even when everything goes well, the airplane is off-course 90 percent of the time! According to pilots, the key is not in learning to make the right decision, but learning when to correct it.

The working mom whose life is flowing smoothly uses the same method. After one error, she feels guilty and makes a correction, that alters her course, then she makes another adjustment which makes her feel guilty, so she makes another correction,... and her kids turn out just fine!

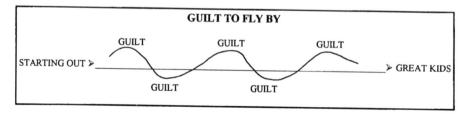

MISTAKES THAT HELP YOUR KIDS

"I can think of nothing more oppressive than a perfect mom.
What normal kid could survive?"

— Sondra

Besides being inevitable, making a mistake is one of the best things you can do for your kids. It is important to keep in mind, "It's not what happens to you, but how you handle what happens to you that's important." It opens the door to a new range of learning experiences for your kids when you show them that you can:

❁ Be Wrong as Well as Right

"It's hard to make mistakes a three-year-old will notice. But sometimes I do something on purpose—like spilling some milk — just so Tommy can see how I handle it."

— Elaine

With older kids, you may not need to make a mistake on purpose: things will come up. Letting your kids see that you take it in stride, even laugh it off, is a great way to model self-confidence. If there are consequences to pay, pay them in good humor. If apologies are in order, apologize. Simply saying "I've been so distracted by work, I haven't given you as much attention as I'd like to lately" can allow you to find out what your child is feeling as well.

A working mom who is overcome with guilt is modeling an inability to cope that isn't helpful to her kids. Trying to show them the extent of her remorse, she may inadvertently be telling them: "Make a mistake and you're ruined! Life is much harder than you can imagine."

❀ Do Things You Don't Want to Do

"One day when I was vacuuming the living room, I happened to mention how tired I was. My four-year-old, Amy, looked up at me in surprise. She couldn't believe I was doing something I didn't want to do. She thought being an adult meant doing whatever you wanted all the time."

— Eliza

Even moms who are dissatisfied and actively looking for ways to spend more time at home can make valuable use of their situation. We all spend time doing things we don't want to do. Whether it's an hour in a tedious math class or a day at a job you dislike, it's something your kids will find especially easy to relate to. With a little effort, you can take the opportunity to show them how to follow through with tolerance and a pleasant attitude.

If they see that even adults have to cope with unpleasant tasks, you may save them the unnecessary guilt caused by the belief that you should never have to do things you don't want to do.

❀ Cope with Delays and Disappointments

"I used to come home after an hour in traffic and vent: 'Sorry I'm late, but some stupid truck had a flat on the freeway and slowed everybody down! You can never get anywhere when you're in a hurry.' Then one day I heard Patricia using the very same words while she was playing. I thought, 'Where on earth did she learn to throw a fit like that?'"

— Candy

Every time your behavior models an adult who can cope with delays and disappointments, you offer your child a skill they can use throughout their lives. Look for healthy, creative ways to express your frustration. And remember — you're being watched.

Mistakes give you a wonderful opportunity to show your kids how to handle the ordinary ups and downs of life. Your maturity will provide a valuable role model as children discover that their own life flows in a pattern that alternates between:

good and bad   *happy and sad*

right and wrong   *lay and work*

rushed and calm   *engaged and bored*

and many gradations in between

* * *

WHAT NEEDS ARE VITAL?

No kid has a fundamental need for you to be infallible, but, according to child guidance clinician, Alfred Adler, one of the strongest drives in kids, or any of us is the need to *belong*. These are vital things, loving, nurturing, and accepting your child. Who can imagine a kid complaining:

"Oh, sure, she *loved* me. I could curl up in her lap if I was scared; I turned to her with my problems; she was always there for me in every way. But she ruined my life. She was just so ... *disorganized!*"

Your child will not be ruined and her self-esteem will not be stunted, if you are not home to provide a "spic and span" home. Bad organization, sloppy housekeeping, and poor cooking techniques are problems, but they will not ruin your kids, nor will your working outside your home. If your kids are really annoyed by those qualities in you, chances are they will excel in those things, usually by way of compensation. In the long run, your way of dealing with those shortcomings will help them face their own.

Developing a strong sense of belonging for your child is far more important. Parent educator Dr. Michael Popkin explains that a parent can cultivate a child's experience of belonging by allowing him to learn and contribute within the family.

In my parenting seminars, I explain that, for children, the family is a small scale version of the world. Within the safety of the family, they can try things out, explore their limits and discover who they are. As a parent, you have the chance to provide your kids with skills that will help them do more than merely survive.

If we were only teaching survival, we could kick kids out of the nest like fledgling birds at a much earlier age. We keep them close to us longer so we can teach them the advanced lessons in how to thrive.

Whether you work or stay home, your love and attention can make the difference between merely surviving and thriving for your kids. As a result, they will gain the self-esteem and courage they need to contend with whatever life brings to them.

* * *

Belonging

It's so essential, yet it is one of the easiest things to convey to your children. Expressing your love through holding, hugging, touching, kissing, playing, laughing, singing—the simplest things—will make your children feel that they belong.

* * *

Learning

When your beliefs and values take hold in your children, you will have tangible evidence that they have not been ruined by the distractions and conflicts of your work. Several ways to help your children learn from you are to:

❀ teach them skills

❀ give them opportunities

❀ show interest in their knowledge

❀ accept their mistakes

Your patience and encouragement will allow them to develop the self-reliance they need to secure their future.

❊ ❊ ❊

Contributing

Working moms on a hectic schedule can easily overlook this one. Letting your children contribute to the family will give you a chance to highlight what valuable, important members of the family they are. Make a point to:

❀ ask for their opinions and feedback

❀ accept their offers of help

❀ acknowledge their cooperation

❀ share responsibilities with them

Some moms do reinforce this idea by holding a regular family meeting where ideas are exchanged and problems hashed out. It is an excellent way to help your kids feel that it is everyone's home and everyone is an active participant. The sense that "we're all in this together" is exactly what you're trying to convey—an unshakable feeling of belonging.

In the difficult teenage years, when kids may feel alienated, special efforts to make them feel that they belong can make all the difference. One mom was accustomed to taking walks on the beach with her friends for half-an-hour a day. In her busy schedule, it was her only real leisure time. She felt her teenage daughter pulling away from her, and I suggested that she take the walk on the beach with her daughter instead of her friends. Seeing the value her mother placed on their connection helped her daughter open up to her. It was a simple thing, but it worked wonders in giving her daughter a sense of belonging.

FAMILY MEETINGS

A lot of moms are put off by the idea of a family meeting. It sounds too deliberate, too formal. "Shouldn't family life just flow?" they wonder. Setting aside a time each week for a meeting brings back memories of being sent to the principal's office as a kid. But a family meeting can be something to look forward to. It's all in your approach.

Some parents make it part of Family Night. Whether it's once a week or once a month, Family Night is written on the calendar and kept sacred. The phone is unplugged. No friends are invited to dinner. No interruptions are allowed. Usually, at each meeting, someone's favorite meal is cooked. After dinner, a meeting — short or long — allows everyone the chance to bring things up. Then the family spends time playing a game or even watching TV together.

When communication in a family is strong, the big questions may well be handled throughout the week as they come up. But a family meeting gives you the perfect opportunity to ask your kids other questions like:

❀ *how can we make better use of the little time we have together?*

❀ *what do you wish we did more often?*

❀ *what do you feel about my working?*

❀ *how important is it to you that I'm home when you get in?*

WHAT DO KIDS REALLY THINK?

Hardly a day goes by that you don't hear that little voice in your head *coaching* you or *scolding* you to tell you know something's gone awry. And 9 times out of 10, your kids have noticed too.

However cool and aloof they seem, kids watch their parents like hawks. They know your every weakness and can spot an inconsistency a mile away. Chances are that before you've even realized that something's wrong, they've already complained about it to their friends. There may even be days when they come right out and say it: "You're ruining my life!" The first time you ask your kids for feedback about how you're doing as a mom, you may be surprised by the response you get.

In a survey by noted child educator Dr. Ray Guarendi's, kids were asked a very direct question: "If 10 is perfect, how would you rate your parents on a 1-to-10 point scale?" The excerpts from their answers are very revealing.

"I would have to give mom and dad an 8 ... A lot of times when the perfect thing to do would have been to say, 'No, we can't afford it,' they would say, 'We'll see if there isn't some way we can work it out.' There were times when they really had work to do and they took time to play with me. They are not perfect, but then perfect people don't need love."

"My parents are now at a 9. As our family matured, they also matured ... It is so much easier to relate to people who are less than perfect ..."

"A 9. I would never say my parents were without fault or that they didn't make mistakes. They let us know that mistakes were just evidence that we had actually tried to do something."

"I would give them a 10 for effort. They have made mistakes, but they are great parents because they really tried."

"I guess an 8. No parents are perfect. If they were, we would never move out of the house!"

Typically, the parents in Dr. Guarendi's survey expected their kids to rank them much lower than they did. Some parents gave all the credit to their kids. When she was rated very highly by her two boys and two girls, one mom asked the ultimate question: "Are we good parents because we have good kids, or are they good kids because we are good parents?"

GIVING IT ALL YOU'VE GOT

In the end, the connection with your child is the key that makes the difference—whether it is forged in precious moments before bedtime by a working mom or during the long, hectic days by a mom who stays at home. More likely than not, that loving connection was what made motherhood appealing in the first place. It's the most important thing to your kids and to you.

In the meantime, it's good to know you have your guilt to keep you on course, sharpen your insights, make you face the things you don't want to see and remind you when you've forgotten. It tempers your dreams with reality and, when you let it, guilt will bring out the best that you have to give. And that's where it all begins!

RECOMMENDED READING FOR MOTHERS

Anderson, Carol M. and Stewart, Susan (1994) *Flying Solo Single Women in Midlife.* New York, NY: Norton Books.

Ash, Mary Kay (1995) *Mary Kay, You Can Have It All.* Rocklin, CA: Primal Publishing.

Bassett, Lucinda (1995) *From Panic to Power.* New York, NY: Harper Collins Publishers.

Bean, Reynold, Ed.M. (1991) *How to Help Your Children Succeed in School.* Los Angeles, CA: Price Stern Sloan, Inc.

Bepko, C. and Krestan, J. (1993) *Singing at the Top of Our Lungs: Women, Love and Creativity.* New York, NY: Harper Collins.

Blanchard, Ken. (1996) *Empowerment Takes More Than a Minute.* San Francisco, CA: Berrett-Koehler Publishers.

Bombeck, Erma (1983) *Motherhood, The Second Oldest Profession.* NewYork, NY: McGraw-Hill Book Company.

Branden, Nathaniel, Ph.D. (1996) *Taking Responsibility.* New York, NY: Simon and Schuster.

Brothers, Joyce, Dr. (1994) *Positive Plus —The Practical Plan for Liking Yourself Better.* New York, NY: Berkley Books.

Bums, David D., M.D. (1993) *Ten Days to Self-Esteem.* New York, NY: Twill.

Burton, Linda and Dittmer, Janet and Loveles, Cheri (1992) *What's A Smart Woman Like You Doing At Home?* Virginia: Mothers at Home.

Carnegie, Dale (1970) *How to Enjoy Your Life and Your Job.* New York, NY: Simon and Schuster.

Craig, J. (1993) *Little Kids, Big Questions: Practical Answers to the Difficult Questions Children Ask About Life.* New York, NY: Hearst Books.

DuBrin, Andrew J. (1995) *Getting It Done.* Pacesetter Books.

Ferrucci, Piero (1982) *What We May Be.* Los Angeles, CA: J. P. Tarcher, Inc.

Gaylin, Willard, M.D. (1979) *Feelings.* New York, NY: Harper & Row, Publishers.

Hartley, Hermine (1990) *The Family Book of Manners.* Ohio: Barbour & Co.

Hobfoll, Stevan, Ph. D. and Hobfoll, Yvonne, Ph.D. (1994) *Work Won't Love You Back.* New York, NY: W.H. Freeman and Company

Jeffers, Susan, Ph.D. (1993) *Feel the Fear and Do It Anyway.* New York, NY: Fawcett Books.

King, Larry (1994) *How to Talk to Anyone, Anytime, Anywhere.* New York, NY: Crown Trade Paperbacks.

Kottler, J.A. (1994) *Beyond Blame.* San Francisco,CA: Jossey Bass.

Lague, L. (1995) *Working Mothers Book of Hints and Tips.* Princeton, NJ: Peterson's.

Landers, Ann (1996) *Wake Up and Smell the Coffee: Advice, Wisdom, and Uncommon Sense.* New York, NY: G.K.Hall & Co.

Lansky, Vicki, (1995) *101 Ways to Be a Special Mom.* Chicago, IL: Contemporary Books.

Mackoff, Barbara, Dr. (1984) *Leaving the Office Behind.* New York, NY: Dell Publishing.

McWilliams, Margaret (1993) *Nutrition For The Growing Years.* Redondo Beach, CA: Plycon Press.

Metzroth, Jane P. (1984) *Picking the Perfect Nanny: A Foolproof Guide to the Best At-Home Childcare.* New York, NY: Simon and Schuster, Inc.

Miller, JoAnn and Weissman, Susan, M. S.W. (1986) *The Parents Guide to Daycare.* New York, NY: Bantam Books.

Naisbitt, John (1996) *Megatrends 2000.* New York, NY: Avon Books.

Nigro, D. (1995) *Working Moms On the Run Manual.* NewYork, NY: Master Media.

Packer, Alex J., Ph.D. (1995) *365 Ways to Love Your Child.* New York, NY: Dell Publishing.

Price, S. C. and Price, T. (1994) *The Working Parents Help Book.* Princeton, New Jersey: Peterson's.

Saavedra, Beth Wilson, (1995) *Meditations for Mothers of Toddlers.* New York, NY: Workman Publishing.

Savage, Terry (1991) *Terry Savage Talks Money.* Chicago, IL: First Harper Perennial.

Schaefer, C.E., and DiGeronimo, T. F. (1994) *How to Talk to Your Kids About Really Important Things: Specific Questions, Answers and Useful Things to Say.* San Francisco, CA: Jossey-Bass.

Scott, Cynthia, D.Ph.D., M.P.H. and Jaffe, Dennis T., Ph.D. (1989) *Managing Personal Change.* Los Altos, CA: Crisp Publications, Inc.

Sinetar, Marsha (1995) *To Build The Life You Want, Create the Work You Love.* New York, NY: St. Martin's Press.

Spock, Benjamin, M.D. (1988) *Dr. Spock on Parenting.* New York, NY: Simon & Schuster.

Sugar, M. H. (1994) *When Mothers Work, Who Pays?* Westport, CT: Bergin & Garvey

Taffel, Ron, Ph.D. (1993) *Parenting by Heart.* New York, NY: Addison-Wesley Publishing Co.

Tamien, Deborah (1994) *Talking From 9 to 5.* New York, NY: Avon Books.

Tieger, Paul and Barron, Barbara-Trieger (1992) *Do What You Are.* Canada: Little, Brown and Company.

Van Buren, Abigail (1989) *The Best of Dear Abbey.* Chicago, IL: Andrews & McMeel.

Waitley, Denis (1979) *The Psychology of Winning.* Chicago, IL: Nightingale-Conant Corp.

Wilson Schaef, Anne (1990). *Laugh! I Thought I'd Die (If I Didn't).* New York, NY: Ballantine Books.

Winston, Stephanie (1978) *Getting Organized.* New York, NY: Warner Books.

Wycoff, Joyce, with Tim Richardson (1995) *Transformation Thinking.* New York, NY: Berkley Books.

Index

Would you like to participate in future research?
WORKING MOTHERS' QUESTIONAIRE

Your Name: (First)_____(Last) _____Date: _____

(Optional

Respond to the following questions:

Then:

1. Did your mother work when you were growing up?

2. What is your birth order?

3. What was your role in your family of origin (i.e., caretaker?)

4. What were your feelings about growing up in your family of origin?

5. Did you look forward to having children of your own?

6. How many?

7. What were your parents' expectations of you for your future?

❖ ❖ ❖

Now:

1. What is your age?

2. What is your occupation now?

3. How many children do you have?

4. Did you work when your children were born? What was your occupation?

5. How much time did you take for maternity leave?

6. What was your company's policy on maternity?

7. What one dominant feeling did you get and from whom?

8. What emotional support did you get and from whom?

9. Did your role in your family change as a result of your first child?

10. Can you describe any feelings of guilt or conflicting feelings you may have had about working and leaving your children?

11. How did you set boundaries for your children when they were young and you were working?

12. Would you have changed anything about your working/child rearing?

13. a. What do you feel now about working? Child rearing?
    b. What do you get most out of working? Child rearing?

14. Who do you rely on most for help with your children?

15. What caregiving arrangements do you have? Are you satisfied?

16. What do you do about illness—yours and theirs?

17. What support do you get from your place of work?

18. What would you change?

19. What three things do you feel most guilty about?

20. Is guilt a positive force in your life? How?

21. Any additional comments?

Mail to:

Muriel S. Savikas, Ph.D.
Post Office Box 3575
Manhattan Beach, CA 90266
or
E-Mail to: DrMuriel@aol.com
or
Call (310) 545-9350 for a telephone interview
with Dr. Savikas

THE COUNSELING and MEDIATION INSTITUTE

Dr. Muriel Savikas, Director

❑ MEDIATION SERVICES: You don't have to fight to win! Avoid costly litigation with your spouse, partner, employer, or others through "dispute resolution" in a balanced, cooperative atmosphere where all parties express their needs in order to negotiate win-win agreements.

"For years I have seen the devastating effects of ligated divorce on families and on children in particular. My desire is to avert the damage with a mediation process that allows the parties' self-esteem to remain in tact."

— Dr. Muriel Savikas

❑ COUNSELING SERVICES: Become a knowledgeable, active parent by improving your relationship with your child. Teach your child healthy behavior, productive communication skills, and independence; enhance your child's social/learning skills, and develop a positive sense of self-worth. Recognize developmental problems before they become unmanageable.

❑ EXPERT WITNESS: Dr. Savikas, Ph.D., MFCC, FPPR, consults with family law attorneys on assessment, treatment and development issues of infants and children. She conducts custody evaluations, psychological and neuropsychological testing and therapy.

SEMINARS — WORKSHOPS — CONSULTING

Dr. Muriel Savikas
Counseling and Mediation Institute
868 Manhattan Beach Blvd., Suite 2
Manhattan Beach, CA 90266
(310) 545-9350 (Phone),   (310) 546-0013 (Fax)
E-Mail: DrMuriel@aol.com

ORDER FORM

	Fax orders:	(310) 546-0013
	Telephone orders	(888) GO-4-P101 Have your VISA or MASTERCARD ready
	Postal orders:	CMI Publishing Post Office Box 3575 Manhattan Beach, CA 90266

Please send the following:

☐ Guilt is Good: What Working Moms Need to Know $14.95

☐ How to be a Better Parent Affirmation Cards $7.95

☐ Gold Parent-Child Pin $12.00

Item	Price	How Many	Subtotal

Shipping and Handling	
$4.00 for the first book	Subtotal
$2.00 for each additional book	Shipping
	CA residents ADD 8.25% TAX
$2.95 for pin/card (up to 4 items)	**TOTAL**

Charge my: ☐ VISA   ☐ MASTERCARD   ☐ CHECK ENCLOSED

Card #: _____ **Exp.** _____

Signature: _____

Name: _____

Address: _____

City: _____ State: _____ ZIP: _____

Telephone: Day_____ Evening _____

Fax: _____ E-Mail: _____